THE DANUBE CYCLE WAY
DONAUESCHINGEN TO BUDAPEST

John and Andrea aboard the Schlögen ferry

ABOUT THE AUTHOR

John Higginson has been a long-distance fell walker for many years. Having been a keen cyclist in his youth, he took up long-distance cycling in Europe a few years after he retired from the post of headmaster of a Cheshire primary school. He is now a writer and lecturer.

He and his wife, Andrea, who have also cycled both south-to-north and east-to-west across France and the length of the medieval pilgrimage route from Le Puy in France to Santiago de Compostela in north-west Spain, spent more than a year researching the historical traditions and the geography of the Danube Cycle Way before embarking on the journey that is described in this book.

John Higginson has also written *The Way of St James – Le Puy to Santiago, a Cyclists' Guide* (Cicerone, 1999).

THE DANUBE CYCLE WAY
DONAUESCHINGEN TO BUDAPEST

by
John Higginson

photographs by Andrea Higginson

2 POLICE SQUARE, MILNTHORPE, CUMBRIA LA7 7PY
www.cicerone.co.uk

ISBN 1 85284 345 4

A catalogue record for this book is available from the British Library.

DEDICATION

In memory of my mother

With thanks to
Andrea, Armin and Rosemarie, without whose help, encouragement
and companionship the journey would not have been made.

ADVICE TO READERS

Readers are advised that while every effort is taken by the author to ensure the accuracy of this guidebook, changes can occur which may affect the contents. It is advisable to check locally on transport, accommodation, shops, etc, but even rights of way can be altered.

The publisher would welcome notes of any such changes.

Front cover: Town centre sculpture, Mengen (Stage 3)

CONTENTS

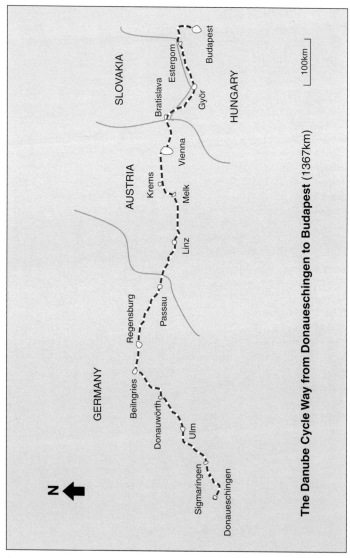

The Danube Cycle Way from Donaueschingen to Budapest (1367km)

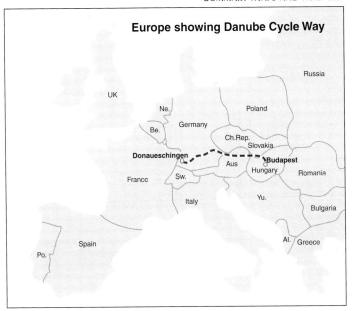

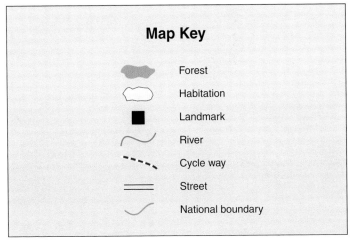

Reflections in the blue pool, Blaubeuren (Stage 4)

INTRODUCTION

Any cyclist living in mainland Europe would almost certainly know the Danube Cycle Way as one of the most popular cycle routes on the Continent. In high season parts of it can be so busy that it is virtually impossible to use it without meeting groups of fellow cyclists every few minutes. Yet the route is little known to Britons and rarely cycled by them. A large part of the route is furnished with well-signed and mostly paved cycleways divorced from vehicular traffic and the whole route takes in four countries – Germany, Austria, Slovakia and Hungary – with lovely scenery and fascinating villages, towns and cities. It is therefore high time that British cyclists got to know the route and enjoyed the outstanding facilities it has to offer. This book aims to introduce the Danube Cycle Way and to give some insight into the people and places encountered on a journey along its length.

The Danube Cycle Way is an ideal 'starter' for cycle touring, especially in Europe. It is flat so the rhythm of daily stages tends to be the same, the whole route is more than adequately provided with places to stay, there must be an information point every 10km along the way, and the route is well used so that anyone with a problem would find help almost immediately. It really is a 'family' route. Most of the cycleway is on dedicated cycle tracks and, therefore, safe. There are no sustained climbs that could exhaust a young rider. There is a lot to see and do when not cycling and there are plenty of like-minded people to meet. (We cycled alongside a German family with an eight-year-old boy, from Vienna to Budapest, and he led the way!) The whole route has 20 stages of about a day but, allowing for days off, a month is a more feasible time-span to complete the whole journey. Many cyclists split this in half and cover the whole route in two trips of a fortnight each, Passau being the ideal 'halfway' mark.

BACKGROUND

The River Danube officially begins its life as a spring bubbling to the surface in the little German town of Donaueschingen. It passes from the edge of the Black Forest through Bavaria before crossing into Austria near Passau. It then winds its way through hilly country on its journey to Vienna before meandering lazily through flat farmland as it becomes the border between Slovakia and Hungary. Finally it swings round the famous 'Golden Bend' before dividing Hungary's capital Budapest. The river continues to the Black Sea but, as a result of political problems

Main Street, Donauwörth (Stage 5)

involving border crossings, the Danube Cycle Way effectively ends in Budapest – after a distance of more than 1350km.

PREPARATION

For seasoned European travellers the Danube Cycle Way is a pleasant, simple route that should not cause any undue problems.

To get the best from the journey, however, it is worth putting in a certain amount of preparation. The route is not as physically or mentally demanding as, say, the Way of Saint James through France and Spain but reasonably fit, informed cyclists will enjoy the Danube Cycle Way so much more. This guide will give you an idea of what to expect.

Cycles

It is not unusual to see people, particularly from the Netherlands, bowling along the Danube Cycle Way on ancient 'sit-up-and-beg' cycles with few or no gears. This is because the way is predominantly flat (in fact it descends 575m in the 1367km from Donaueschingen to Budapest) and no long severe hill need be encountered if you stick rigidly to the prescribed route. However some places close to the trail which are worth a visit are at the end of lengthy ascents of the valley sides, some of which are quite steep. There are also long straight sections which, if wind assisted, could afford some high-speed travelling! With these things in mind, a set of

seven gears (11-26) on a triple chain ring (42/32/22) or similar will in general provide all the gearing necessary for this journey.

This is one of the few European routes where touring cycles with drop-handlebars are rarely seen. The majority of mainland Europeans use town cycles with straight bars for the journey and, as there is some off-road cycling to be done (though nothing too long or severe), mountain bikes and hybrids are the next most popular cycles on the trail. In my own case a pair of American Trek hybrid trail cycles were used for the journey equipped with medium-range gears and Panaracer Passela kevlar tyres. The result was easy long-distance cycling, my wife and I suffering only one puncture each on the entire return journey. It is worth noting that because the terrain has little variation for long stretches, a comfortable riding position to prevent severe stiffness and soreness is essential. Straight handlebars can cause numbness of the hands, arms and shoulders on long journeys but a judiciously adjusted pair of bar-ends can alleviate much of this discomfort, allowing the hand position to be changed regularly.

Equipment

Climatic conditions are not likely to be as extreme as those encountered in, say, the Pyrenees, the Cantabrian Mountains or the Alps but during our journey in July and August we had only five dry days out of 40 and the weather was cold and windy enough to demand hot drinks at regular intervals! It is these very variable conditions that dictate the equipment necessary for the journey.

A pair of totally waterproof panniers and a similar bar-bag are absolutely essential. There is nothing worse than arriving at an overnight halt to find that everything in your bag is soaking wet. Our bags were expensive but for this sort of journey, where the weather is so unpredictable, they are worth the outlay.

Similarly, lightweight breathable waterproof clothing that does not become clammy and cold after several hours' continuous cycling is a must. When travelling alongside the water's edge in high gusty winds, a cape is not a wise choice. Whilst capes do allow the wind to pass over the body, keeping it free from perspiration, their propensity to act as a sail when cycling less than a metre from the edge of a deep, fast-flowing river makes them too dangerous to seriously contemplate on this particular trail.

Flies and midges can be a severe problem. Whilst cycling, a pair of tight-fitting glasses will keep eyes protected and, in the evening, either mosquito repellent or a net should ensure a good night's sleep.

This is more of a family holiday route than one cycled by lycra-clad enthusiasts so clothing tends to be T-shirt and padded shorts rather than race-wear. (However no one will stare at you whatever you turn out in!)

It is essentially a journey to be enjoyed, so comfort dictates. There are places along the route where the cycleway is used by pedestrians and roller-blade enthusiasts as well as cyclists, when there is always the possibility of cyclists being unseated. Wearing a helmet along the whole route is therefore strongly advised.

There are few hostels on this route but bed and breakfast accommodation is both plentiful and cheap (often little different in price from that of hostels). It is therefore debatable whether there is any need to carry sleeping bags (they take up a lot of room and may never be opened) or cooking equipment (though a small electric travel kettle with continental adapter is useful).

Basic tools, including a small jar of Swarfega, should be carried for emergencies, as should a pump, but almost every small town on the way (several can be found each day) has a cycle shop manned by helpful, knowledgeable staff (the one in Passau is even open 24 hours a day). There are also large numbers of cyclists on this trail and they can be relied on to swarm to your assistance should the need arise.

A full kit list of items you may wish to consider taking with you can be found in Appendix B.

Maps and Route-Finding

I have yet to find a good set of compatible maps for the whole route. Road maps like the Michelin 1:400,000

Central Square, Bratislava (Stage 16)

The Danube 'break-through' between Kelheim and Weltenburg (Stage 8)

number 984 (Germany) do not show the cycleway clearly enough, and walkers' maps are often too detailed and you have to purchase and carry too many of them. The best and most detailed maps are to be found in the *Donau-Radweg* books published by Bikeline (see Bibliography). There are three books covering the whole route though the first and third are only published in German. This does not of course affect the maps, which are clear and accurate though not always precisely up-to-date. Unfortunately local authorities make a habit of changing the route or repositioning signs throughout their region and this can cause considerable confusion. If you are in doubt anywhere it is better to ask a local inhabitant rather than a fellow cyclist who may be just as lost as you are. However with these books you are unlikely to get seriously lost.

I could find no suitable detailed map for the Altmühl Trail (Stages 6–8 in this guide) and had to rely on one advertising supermarkets in the area that I found in a local tourist office! That said, the signing along this stretch was exceptionally clear and there were no route-finding difficulties in this region at all.

When finding your way in Slovakia and Hungary be prepared to find that road signs, if they exist, particularly in towns and cities, may be written in Cyrillic script, which does not match the names found on maps. Also remember that a minor road in these countries may not be paved and

could easily turn out to be little more than a muddy track. Signing of the trail throughout Hungary is very intermittent. The Michelin Map 925 – Hungary (1:400,000) is perfectly adequate to give an overview of the journey for the purposes of route planning through Slovakia and Hungary but do not expect to find the cycleway marked on it – or even many of the minor roads.

Finding your way round most of the larger cities should not pose a problem – just follow signs to the *Centrum* (town centre). Tourist information centres in Donaueschingen, Regensburg, Passau, Linz, Vienna, Györ and Budapest all provide good detailed maps that are ideal for exploring the cities on foot or by cycle. (The exception is Bratislava, where you may have difficulty even finding the tourist office!) Note also that, whichever maps are used, the exit from Vienna is likely to prove a challenge.

See the Bibliography for a list of maps.

Fitness

Peak fitness for this route is not essential. Depending on the time you have, distances can be tailored to your needs. Accommodation is plentiful enough that any day can easily be curtailed. Remember, however, that on most mornings you will have to climb back onto your trusty steed and cycle for several hours, and that sometimes there may be a headwind

Radstationen (cyclists' information bureaux) are situated along the route

all day, so stamina is more important on this journey than strength. Some sections of the route are exposed and this can result in hard pedalling into a wind that is funnelled up the river valley, even though overall the route may be descending. It is advisable to start cycling a few miles at home each day prior to commencing the journey, increasing the distance gradually until, before departure, a string of journeys exceeding 80km per consecutive day does not seem too daunting.

For most of the journey the route runs along the bottom of the Danube Valley, but if you wish to cycle to the panoramic viewpoints such as monasteries or castles that you can see off the trail it will usually entail some quite severe climbing, and this should be taken into consideration when planning the day. Try not to arrive at your overnight accommodation totally exhausted or you will not want to travel at all the next day!

Accommodation

The Danube Cycle Way is used by many people as a long-distance holiday route so there is no shortage of accommodation anywhere along it. Hostels (*Herbergen*), private rooms (*Zimmer*), guesthouses (*Gasthöfe, Pensionen*) and hotels (*Hotels*) are plentiful. That said, they can be busy or full in high season as many Germans and Dutch make block bookings at hotels months in advance and many places are filled by groups of cyclists who are riding together, so it pays to think ahead a little. In general prices are lower than in Britain for similar standards of accommodation, the lowest prices being in Slovakia and Hungary.

In many ways booking more than a few hours ahead spoils the adventure and may prevent time being spent at unexpected discoveries along the route because a pre-booked accommodation must be reached by nightfall. You can book ahead en route at tourist offices or at the special *Radstationen* (cyclists' information bureaux) found at regular intervals along the way and especially in Austria. The latter are very helpful and have lists of overnight accommodation geared to cyclists' needs. If you are doubtful about making yourself understood on the telephone some will make the booking for you. If you do not book ahead try to arrive at your destination before 6pm as accommodation is usually full by then and many tourist offices in towns and villages close at this time.

In Hungary (particularly Budapest) people offering different types of accommodation may accost you in the street and particularly at railway stations. This is quite normal and legal but be prepared to haggle and do not accept lavish accommodation that you do not want. There are several tourist offices that have the addresses of pensions – basic rooms but clean and extremely good value.

Apart from international youth hostels there are in Germany a number of *Naturfreundehausen*. These are superior hostels with restaurants attached that are usually set in fine scenery or even nature parks, though they often charge no less than bed and breakfast accommodation.

In Vienna, where cheap accommodation may seem scarce, the Viennese Tourist Office produces an excellent accommodation guide in which even the least expensive *Pensionen* are both clean and comfortable. At railway stations there, students offer leaflets advertising hostels for overnight accommodation in the city. These are perfectly adequate but bear in mind that they may be crowded, noisy and filled with excited young people!

Although it is possible to find campsites along the whole of the route, there are a number of factors against camping. It is little cheaper than simple bed and breakfast accommodation, and unreliable weather means the unpleasant prospect of having to pitch or strike tents in pouring rain as well as having to pack and carry wet camping equipment. However many campsites do offer cheap chalet accommodation and this too can be ascertained at the *Radstationen* along the way.

HOW TO GET THERE AND BACK (INCLUDING RIVER CROSSINGS)

There is no direct route from Britain to Donaueschingen by public transport. The simplest and most convenient way to arrive at the start of the

Danube Cycle Way in Donaue-schingen is via the European Bike Express (see Appendix C) and German Railways.

The Bike Express is a fully equipped coach and cycle-trailer that takes cyclists from any one of a number of pick-up points throughout England, starting at Middlesbrough, as far as Basle. If coming from Scotland you can travel down to Middlesbrough and stay overnight there before boarding the Express the following morning. From Ireland you could take the ferry to Holyhead and then the train to Leeds to meet the Express there. Cheap overnight accommodation is available at the drop-off point, a few kilometres from the centre of Basle city, then from Badischer Bahnhof station in Basle, Donaueschingen is only one change (at Singen) and a couple of hours away by train.

If you choose to travel at the weekend, the cost of any journey on German Railways for up to five people is only about £14 per day in total. Cycles may be extra. (Remember this when planning your return journey.)

As a general rule, cycles and planes do not mix. There are so many horror stories of damaged bikes being found on airport carousels and demands for extra payment not mentioned when the booking was made, and it is difficult to find cheap flights home to the UK from Budapest or Vienna. Rail travel is by far the easiest and cheapest option.

Much of the River Danube is navigable by quite large vessels beyond Kelheim. In fact the short stretch from Kelheim to Weltenburg *should* be made by boat as there is no other way to see the spectacular scenery there. There are many crossings of the river to be made and often this entails taking a ferry. These are cheap and frequent and used to carrying loaded cycles but there may not be a strict timetable. Crossings can also be made over most of the huge dams that will be found straddling the river at regular intervals. These are free of tolls for cyclists but may have restricted crossing times (you can check in advance by asking at the *Radstation*).

The return journey may provide a few unexpected hazards. In theory buses from Budapest to Vienna carry cycles but in practice they do not! To take the train, book at least one day in advance and expect a wait of at least an hour to receive your 11 pieces of paper which allow you to take yourself and your cycle out of Hungary. Have your passport and as much other identity as you can find with you. Show them, but if at all possible DO NOT let them out of your sight.

Travel by train from Vienna is much simpler, but a more pleasant way to travel is on the river itself. One afternoon and evening's sail will take you and your cycle through some of the most spectacular scenery between Linz and Passau and the cost should not break the bank.

Passau from the Veste Oberhaus Castle (Stage 10)

Using the cheap weekend travel offer it is possible to travel the 880km from Passau to Basle (including five changes, all carefully documented and planned by German Railways) for the same rate as the short journey from Basle to Donaueschingen – less than £20 for two people and two cycles!

WHAT TO EXPECT ON THE JOURNEY

Food

There is a European saying, 'Breakfast like a king, lunch like a prince and dine like a pauper'. This tends to be the eating habit of most cyclists along this route. Breakfasts, particularly in Bavaria, tend to be large and lengthy with cooked meats, cheese, eggs, pastries, bread and cakes as well as cereal, fruit juice, yoghurt and coffee or tea. What you cannot eat is often handed to you in a bag to take on your journey! Lunches, which are often cooked, consist of soup, a meat dish (frequently with dumplings) and a cake, usually accompanied by beer. Evening meals are, by contrast, quite light consisting of a toasted snack or an omelette. Although wine is available everywhere, particularly in the Wachau region of Austria, beer is more commonly drunk or, in eastern Austria, the apple and pear drink known as *Most*.

In general the cost of food is low. In supermarkets it is very cheap and that served in cafés or restaurants is considerably cheaper than the same meal served in the United Kingdom. In Slovakia and Hungary

19

the meals and drinks are embarrassingly cheap. Hungarian meals tend to be hearty with some form of stew and dumplings being the main constituents. Hungarians like highly spiced food and a savoury dish will often include fine slices of a greenish-yellow pimento – even at breakfast. This appears to be the hottest substance known to man and should be taken (if at all) in great moderation! Watching foreigners eating it provides locals with a great deal of merriment.

In season, fruit is very plentiful. Huge pyramids of watermelons and trays of peaches and apricots are to be found for sale along the cycleway. Once again they are very cheap but of the highest quality. Like the Austrians, Hungarians enjoy large sticky cakes and these are often served at the end of a meal. Both beer and wine are readily available at very low prices throughout Slovakia and Hungary.

Language

If you are told that English is now the universally accepted and spoken language throughout Europe, do not believe it. Whilst many Germans and Austrians in large cities or in official buildings such as tourist offices or banks do speak English, many villagers do not and much of this journey is through tiny villages. In Hungary locals frequently speak German as well as their mother tongue but very few speak English. In Slovakia, Czech is spoken and little else so be prepared to wave your

arms, nod or shake your head and smile a lot! That said, this journey is there to be enjoyed so do not worry about possible difficulties – struggling with the language is one way of getting to know the locals. They will appreciate your efforts and will not harangue you for making mistakes.

The River Danube is given different names depending on which country it is flowing through and its local name has been used throughout this guide: the Donau in Austria and Germany, the Dunaj in Slovakia and the Duna in Hungary.

Money

On this journey, cash talks. Credit and debit cards are not readily accepted and the best way to obtain the currency of the country you are passing through is via the automatic cash dispensers found outside banks in most large towns. Unfortunately in Germany these may not accept your card on Sundays or even Saturdays (they are available only to locals). Most bed and breakfast establishments expect to be paid in cash and many hotels and restaurants, especially in Slovakia, seem reluctant to accept plastic.

Since the arrival of the Euro this coinage is universally accepted in Germany and Austria and may be accepted in Slovakia and Hungary alongside those countries' own coinage. However exchange rates may be poor and care should be taken to shop around and only change money at authorised outlets. When crossing from one country to another there are official currency exchange offices at the border but these do not always offer a good rate of exchange and it may be worth shopping around in the first large town you come to. Do not even think of making a deal with anyone on the street who may approach you offering to change money, though this is likely to happen regularly in the Eastern European countries. This form of exchange is illegal and even if you are not arrested you are likely to be badly ripped off.

In most countries the currency of a neighbouring one is often accepted close to the border but the exchange rate may be very poor.

Flora and Fauna

Through much of Germany the route travels either through intensively farmed land where wild flowers such as poppies and ragwort grow on the borders of fields or through wooded limestone gorges where scabius and wood anemones abound. In Austria, where woodland again dominates, there are occasional meadows of wild flowers including snake grass and periwinkle. Orchards produce breath-taking displays of fruit blossom in spring. In Hungary, where farming is less intensive, fields of wild flowers dance among the grass, still grown for hay and as pasture for horses.

The skies are dominated by birds of prey, particularly buzzards, which can be heard 'mewing' overhead. In the woodlands small mammals such as martens can be seen crossing the cycleway and occasionally deer can be heard and sometimes seen near the track.

Vineyards in the Wachau (Stage 13)

The Schönbrunn Palace, Vienna (Stage 15)

TOPOGRAPHY

Essentially this route follows a river valley from its source towards its mouth. This means that for most of the journey the way is downhill or at least relatively flat. However the Danube, in common with most other rivers, flows between quite high hills so any diversion from it may entail a good deal of serious climbing. The positive side of this, however, is that whereas roads may divert from the riverbank the cycleway hugs it almost all the time, reducing the climbing to a minimum. As a result mileages on this journey are quite high though they still allow plenty of time to stop and admire the scenery and architecture.

Having left the Black Forest at its source the Danube is soon flowing through limestone country (Stage 1). Evidence of this is everywhere, both at ground level, where the river sinks beneath its bed to be resurrected some distance further on, and on the skyline, where pinnacles of rock thrust heavenwards creating grotesque silvery shapes crowned with castles, churches and crosses. Nowhere is this more evident than in the section around Beuron (Stage 2). By departing from the banks of the Danube to visit the strange phenomena in Blaubeuren (Stage 4), and again to follow the River Altmühl to Kelheim (Stages 6–8), the limestone scenery is maintained almost as far as Passau (Stage 10).

Once Austria is entered granite dominates the landscape as the river contorts itself, sometimes through 180 degrees, between the hard surrounding hills (Stage 11). This dramatic scenery now continues until the landscape softens as the area known as the Wachau is reached (Stage 13). Here terraced hillsides, which support huge vineyards and orchards, stretch up on both sides of the river, giving the impression of gigantic green and brown staircases.

As Vienna is approached (Stage 15) the scenery is dominated by fluvial forests of aspen trees which line the riverbank before finally giving way to the beautiful Vienna Woods.

Between Vienna and Bratislava (Stage 16) the terrain remains flat until hills again rise as the capital of Slovakia is approached. It is from these hills to the left of the cycleway that the city's highrise apartments can be seen miles away. Beyond Bratislava the hills soon recede as the trail passes through the great alluvial farmlands of Hungary until the 'Golden Bend' is reached, near Esztergom (Stage 19), where the south bank of the river is dominated by the Visegrad mountains. Once more the hills to the south become less severe as Budapest is reached (Stage 20).

HOW TO USE THIS GUIDE

The whole of the journey from Donaueschingen to Budapest has been divided into 20 cycling stages of varying lengths depending to some extent on the topography but more so on the time necessary to visit places en route. These divisions are purely arbitrary and need not be followed slavishly. You may choose, if you like, to treat each stage as a day's cycling but there are so many possible places to stay along the way that any stage can be lengthened or shortened according to your whim.

Towns and villages along the Danube Cycle Way have been set **in bold type** so they can be used as a guide when route planning. Each significant township has a line to itself. The number of metres printed after it is its height above sea level, and the

St Stephen

There are two St Stephens associated with this journey. The first saint is revered in Germany and Austria as the first Christian martyr. Stephen was a Greek-speaking Jew renowned for his eloquence. He was a contemporary and friend of the apostles, trusted with the gathering and distribution of alms. Stephen was put to death by stoning (a wonderful depiction of this is found in the cathedral in Vienna) – perhaps this is why he is the patron saint of headaches.

The second saint is associated with Hungary. He was a king who lived and died around Estergom, having been crowned there in the year 1000AD. Statues of the saint can be found throughout the country, notably in Pest Cathedral and in Buda, outside the church of St Matthias.

Parliament Building in Budapest (Stage 20)

numbers in brackets indicate the number of kilometres travelled from Donaueschingen followed by the number of kilometres to Budapest. The information in brown type is a guide to what can be found in each town. Available facilities are shown in *green italic*, followed by a brief description of places of interest to visit.

As most of this journey is along dedicated cycle tracks, few roads or road numbers are mentioned. Even in large towns and cities cycleways are used, rendering descriptions of road junctions irrelevant. The river is important, however, and wherever possible crossing places are made clear. The terms 'left' and 'right' bank refer to the side of the river when cycling towards Budapest (downstream).

The accompanying route maps are there to give a flavour of each stage

you are to travel. River crossing places are shown as are the towns and villages along the way. The scale is only approximate but the overall distance to be travelled on that stage of the cycleway is accurate. The town plans show the route of the cycleway into and out of the major towns and cities and a simple route into the town centre. Larger scale, highly detailed town plans can be purchased on arrival from local tourist offices.

Finally, remember that this route is there to be explored and enjoyed at a leisurely pace. There are many families with small children who use parts of the track as a pleasant walk and, as mentioned, in places there are numerous roller-blade enthusiasts who swoop around the walkers and cyclists. With care, everyone can enjoy this route.

Donaueschingen 677m (0/1367)
All facilities
This is a pleasant little town on the edge of the Black Forest with brightly painted houses and a smart town hall. Its claim to fame, the Donauquelle, or Danube Spring, is to be found on the edge of the town in the grounds of the Fürstenberg Schloß, a small palace surrounded by parkland. The water that bubbles to the surface here flows through a grating and forms a narrow stream that joins a river, the Brigach, after a hundred metres. This river immediately changes its name and becomes the Danube, or Donau as it will be called for the next thousand kilometres. A notice here says that the spring is 678m above sea level and 2840km from its mouth.

Musicians' Statue, Donaueschingen

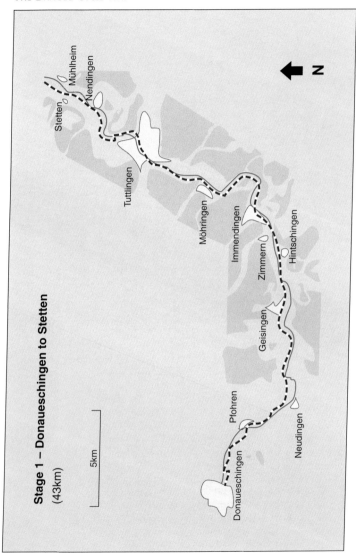

Stage 1 – Donaueschingen to Stetten
(43km)

5km

N

Mühlheim
Nendingen
Stetten
Tuttlingen
Möhringen
Immendingen
Zimmern
Hintschingen
Geisingen
Pfohren
Neudingen
Donaueschingen

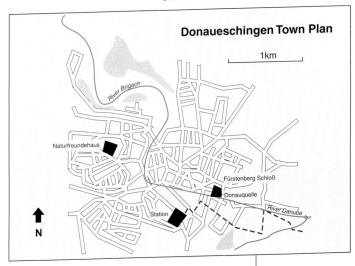

Donaueschingen Town Plan

Push your cycles across the well-manicured gravel to the river and stay on its left bank for 200m before crossing the bridge onto its right bank following the *Donauradweg* (Danube Cycle Way) signs. Do not be surprised if you find you have cycled round in a circle here as the signs can be confusing.

The cycleway, which has a fine surface, soon leaves the river and wanders across farmland with occasional light industry until it reaches

Pfohren 675m (6/1361)

Campsite, pool, cycle shop, medieval fortress, art gallery
This is a pretty village with some attractive wooden houses. Here the Donau is crossed onto its left bank. Sporadic outbreaks of light industry are still to be found along the way until **Neudingen**, with its Fürstenberg tomb and park, is sighted on the far bank of the river.

Although you have been riding virtually on the flat since Donaueschingen, the cycleway now begins to climb as it rounds a conical hill to the left before descending to enter the small town of

Geisingen 667m (16/1351)

All facilities, nature reserve of forest and meres

In the centre of this pleasant town, cross the railway and follow it closely until the cycleway crosses the Donau and swings right to the edge of the village of

Hintschingen 675m (19/1348)

Cycle shop, shelter

The trail now sweeps left below the village to join and cross the Donau opposite the village of

Zimmern 664m (20/1347)

Hotel, guesthouse

The route now runs alongside the railway line until it reaches the wood-yard and railway station at

Immendingen 652m (22/1345)

Information, hotel, guesthouses, cycle shop

It is impossible to miss the brightly painted town hall, and the local museum is worth a brief visit.

In the centre of town, cross the railway via the footbridge, cycle past the highly decorated town hall and follow the clear signs that take you round the houses to avoid the main road before recrossing the Donau with the railway on the right.

The next crossing of the Donau in a couple of kilometres is via a covered bridge built of wood (a good shelter if the weather is inclement). These are quite common and very picturesque. Soon afterwards a sign will be seen to the right indicating a country park with picnic facilities and toilets. Here begins a strange section of the Donau where the river begins to disappear and reappear a number of times beneath its limestone bed (known as the *Donauversinkung*). Do not be tempted to cycle on the slippery, muddy track along the right bank of the river to see this as it can be narrow and quite dangerous in wet weather. Go back to the cycle trail, where a kilometre later a second sign directs visitors to a totally dry section of the Donau riverbed where it is possible to walk

right across the river without getting your feet even damp! The trail now follows the Donau closely and the same phenomenon is sighted several times before the river re-emerges fully at

Disappearing Danube (Donauversinkung) beyond Immendingen

Möhringen 650m (31/1336)
Information, hotel, gîte, guesthouses, rooms, cycle shop
See the old town hall and hunting lodge, and, if you have time, visit the wildlife reserve.

Out of the town the cycleway soon rejoins the left bank of the Donau until it reaches the outskirts of a much larger conurbation. Cross two railway lines and follow the signs over the river before negotiating a busy main road to cycle into the centre of

Tuttlingen 645m (37/1330)
All facilities
A modern high-tech industrial town with a thriving prosperous centre, the German government has invested vast sums of money in Tuttlingen and the whole of this region to promote twenty-first-century industries – and it shows.

Some time should be spent in the old town and the Protestant parish church. The gallery next to the impressive town hall and the Honberg ruins are also worth a visit.

To leave, return to the right bank of the river and at the far edge of the town, cross to the left bank of the river, making a wide sweep, until the railway line is crossed. Follow the latter closely before passing beneath it and rejoining the river close to **Nendingen**. An easy ride now leads into

Stetten 635m (43/1324)
Rooms
If needed, overnight accommodation is available in private *Zimmer* at the top end of the village beyond the school. (Note that the nearest restaurant is in the old picturesque town of **Mühlheim** 2km away, which is certainly worth visiting to see its ancient gateway, ramparts and beautifully preserved houses.)

Bavarian breakfast, Stetten

STAGE 2
Stetten to Ennetach (58km) – Total 101km

Leave Stetten by the cycleway with the river on your right, passing through **Altstadt** (Old Town) which paradoxically is a modern development of bungalows! Looking ahead it is obvious that the valley is beginning to narrow, and by the time the cycleway reaches Fridingen the trail has obviously entered a dramatic limestone gorge.

Fridingen 619m (50/1317)
Information, hotels, guesthouses, rooms, pool, cycle shop
There is a local museum, an interesting castle close to the historic town centre, and St Anne's Chapel. The town is also well known for its local crafts.

On leaving the town, follow the river on the left bank until the trail crosses a bridge. From this point onwards for the rest of this stage the way is surprisingly hilly with short steep inclines, often hidden until the last minute. The surface is often not paved; instead, gravel or shale and sand are used for the top surface. This can prove tricky to negotiate with laden cycles in wet weather and care should be taken. The scenery however is very fine with steep wooded hillsides and great spurs of limestone penetrating towards the sky.

After 8km of beautiful winding tracks the **Fridingen-Jägerhaus** is reached. This is an old hunting lodge that is open both as a wildlife and hunting museum and a tea room at times but do not rely on it. Three kilometres further along the cycleway the trail enters the fascinating old town of

Beuron 610m (61/1306)
Information, hotel, guesthouse
This small town is dominated by its huge Benedictine monastery whose church can be visited when services are not taking place. Here can be heard the Gregorian

Stage 2 – Stetten to Ennetach
(58km)

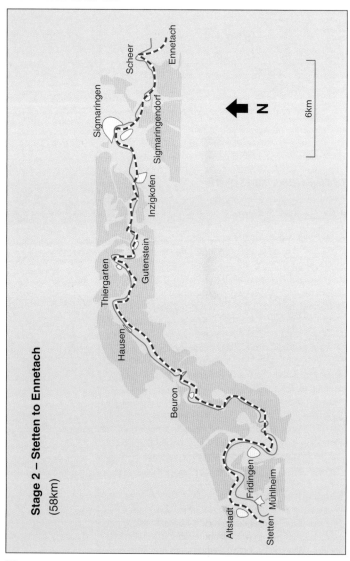

Rock pinnacle with cross near Beuron

Chant sung regularly by members of the community. The interior of the church is covered with Baroque decoration and the gardens are both restful and attractive. Also see the Chapel of St Maurus, the ancient bridge and the exhibition of wildlife along the Donau.

To enter the town and reach the monastery turn left and leave the cycleway at the bridge. Descend a steep hill which swings to the left before climbing again to reach the monastery entrance. On leaving the monastery you climb back up the hill and return to the bridge to regain the cycleway. The gorge continues to fascinate as it winds its way among bizarre rock formations. The cycleway crosses the river a couple more times before the valley widens a little as it reaches the campsite at

Hausen im Tal 594m (69/1298)
Information, hotel, guesthouse, campsite
This is a good spot for a break, with picnic tables and refreshments on hand, although coach parties can make it busy.

The trail continues to hug the right bank of the river, with steep hills particularly to the right, although the river itself widens a little. Being in a nature park the area is teeming with wildlife both on the water and in the woods and it is not unusual to see animals such as deer and otters on the trail. Now you reach

Thiergarten 591m (71/1296)
Hotel, guesthouses, cycle shop, cafes, restaurants
On a tight bend of the river just beyond Thiergarten lies St George's Chapel, the smallest basilica in Europe. After crossing the river just beyond the basilica, the cycleway passes under the railway before recrossing the river as it enters

Gutenstein 590m (79/1288)
Hotel, guesthouse
For the next 5–6km the river valley narrows again, and the cycleway crosses it several times, punctuated by a number of short, steep hills, before it reaches the peaceful retreat of

Inzigkofen 587m (87/1280)
Information, hotel, guesthouse, rooms
There are cloisters and an interesting Bavarian Museum to be seen here as well as the Devil's Bridge and Pulpit Rock viewpoint.

From here on the scenery begins to change substantially. The valley widens and the woodlands recede, being replaced by a series of towns interspersed with arable farmland. Industry also appears, mainly in the form of cement works alongside the railway line, utilising the vast quantities of limestone quarried locally. Soon the

cycleway begins to climb steeply on the approach to the large Bavarian town of

Sigmaringen

Sigmaringen 570m (89/1278)
All facilities, campsite
The bustling old centre of the town is very attractive with its towering castle, narrow streets and squares where cafes and bars spill out onto the pavements. The castle houses the largest collection of weapons in Europe as well as a fine art gallery and a museum of horse-drawn coaches and carriages. The Church of St Johann should be visited. If supplies are needed this is the place to purchase them.

Following the signs, ride down to the banks of the Donau, keeping it to your left. Soon it will begin to meander away from the trail before returning. This will happen several times before it reaches the outskirts of

35

Sigmaringendorf 568m (96/1271)
All facilities
This bustling town at the confluence of the Donau and the Lauchert is famous for its broadleaved deciduous trees that provide brilliant autumn colours. The chapel at the bridge is also interesting, if it is open.

A mere 3km further along the trail, just beyond the paper mill, is the much more attractive little town of

Scheer 561m (99/1268)
Information, hotel, guesthouses
The castle, St Nicholas's Church and Loretto chapel should be visited. An exploration of its narrow streets and winding lanes will prove productive, for here can be found traditional Bavarian architecture on a more human scale.

The exit from **Scheer** is difficult to find as no signs to the cycleway are apparent. The town is built in a tight bend of the Donau and it is very easy to become disorientated. Remember that the Donau should always be to the left of the trail until it is no longer visible. If in doubt leave along the right side of the main road to Mengen, passing large car showrooms to the right, and at the first opportunity cross the railway line then turn left, staying alongside it, with the line to your left.
From this point the cycleway will be a good distance from the river, which cannot be seen. Follow the railway line until the ribbon development is reached that marks the outskirts of

Ennetach 556m (101/1266)
Rooms, restaurant, bar
This small development is a suburb and dormitory town of Mengen. The parish church has a fine square tower, typical of the region, with a brightly coloured tiled roof.

STAGE 3
Ennetach to Dettingen (57km) – Total 158km

The cycleway, along minor roads, is clearly signed into the centre of

Mengen 554m (103/1264)
All facilities
The medieval timber-framed houses and ancient parish church in the town centre, similar to that in Ennetach, are well worth exploring. There is also a local museum. This is a very busy town with a great deal of heavy traffic that needs to be negotiated with great care as there are no cycleways through the town centre. The exit from Mengen, which is not clearly signed, goes through a rather shabby industrial estate before emerging in flat farmland near to the Donau, which can now be seen, lined with trees. Cycling close to the right bank of the river, this is a long flat section through fields of maize with little to divert the eye, eventually leading into the medieval town of

Riedlingen 529m (124/1243)
All facilities
The ancient town centre is very attractive, particularly the Church of St George. The local museum in the old hospital and the house of the Baroque artist Wegscheider should also be visited if time is available. Supermarkets here can provide supplies which may not be available anywhere throughout the rest of this stage.

Leave the town by the same bridge used to enter it and turn left, staying on the right bank of the Donau. The trail continues to cross flat countryside, bridging the river close to **Daugendorf**. There is no need to enter the village however. Instead head through **Bechingen** for the small village of

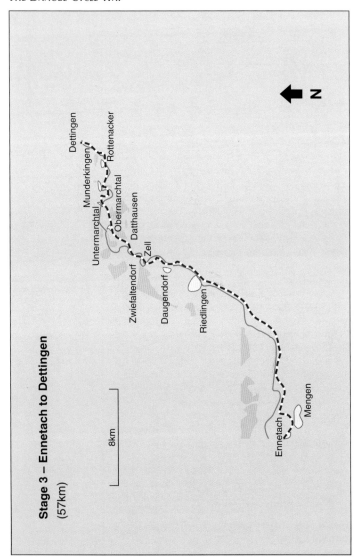

Stage 3 – Ennetach to Dettingen
(57km)

8km

Dettingen
Rottenacker
Munderkingen
Obermarchtal
Untermarchtal
Datthausen
Zwiefaltendorf
Zell
Daugendorf
Riedlingen
Mengen
Ennetach

N

Zell 520m (132/1235)
No facilities
Cross the Donau twice more before cycling into

Zwiefaltendorf 520m (134/1233)
Guesthouses
There is a small castle, a fine Baroque church, a cave
with stalagmites and an interesting water-driven sawmill.

Leave the town beside the railway line on an easy flat
section. The moment the line is crossed, however,
beware! The well-surfaced trail takes a blind right-hand
bend and suddenly climbs very steeply on an extremely
uneven surface. Many unwary cyclists have come to
grief here so be prepared. It is easier and safer to dismount and push your cycle to the top of the hill.

The climb leads through the tiny farming village of
Datthausen to the main road (B311). Do not cross it, as
the sign might imply, but turn left here onto the cycle
track to the right of the road and make a long slow
ascent, crossing the main road just before its summit. It is
not worth taking the cycleway to Rechtenstein which has
nothing of particular interest. Instead keep parallel to the
main road, which is now on the right, and cycle into

Obermarchtal 515m (140/1227)
Information, no other facilities
Visit the much-altered Baroque church and cloisters as
well as the historic soldiers' cemetery.

Following the signs, the way is now across open rolling
farmland with wide horizons as far as

Untermarchtal 508m (145/1222)
Information
St Andrea's Church and the castle can be visited.

Cross the river onto the left bank, although the cycleway does not stay close to it. One kilometre after leaving the town, at a sharp right-hand junction, ignore the

cycleway sign to the right and climb gently straight on for a few hundred metres to the Frauenkirche, a beautiful small Baroque church and convent whose fine restrained decoration is not, for once, over the top. There is an air of peace in this tiny community and no harm can be done by resting here a while. Now retrace the route to the junction and turn left, following the sign, over the railway. The road gradually descends through

Roadside church, Algershofen

Algershofen 510m (148/1219)
No facilities
There is a tiny early church on the roadside which may be open.

Having crossed the river yet again, cycle into the busy little town of

Munderkingen 505m (149/1218)
All facilities
There is a well-preserved historic town centre complete with town hall, timber-framed buildings, Renaissance fountain and the sixteenth-century Gothic Parish Church of St Dionysius which has eighteenth-century Baroque additions.

Cycle into the town centre and at the railway line turn sharp right, passing in front of the station. The river will soon appear on the right but from the point where the trail passes beneath the railway track the cycleway veers to the left across open fields until it descends into

Rottenacker 499m (153/1214)
Information, cycle shop
The fifteenth-century Protestant Church of St Wolfgang should be visited if there is sufficient time.

Follow the signs to turn left at an awkward and haz-ardous junction near the town centre. Having turned left, swing immediately right onto the cycleway to cross both the railway line and, soon after, the Donau, and cycle along its right bank. Soon the tall chimneys of Zellstoff-Fabrik will be seen ahead. They will eventually be passed but before they are reached cross the railway line into

Dettingen 499m (158/1209)
Guesthouse
The area is notorious for its midges!

STAGE 4
Dettingen to Günzburg (60km) – Total 218km

This next part of the journey, as far as Ulm, does not follow the *Donauradweg*. Instead it branches off to visit one of the most unusual and atmospheric towns on the whole itinerary whilst bypassing no place of particular interest.

Recross the railway line and leave **Dettingen** by the roadside cycleway, passing the huge Zellstoff-Fabrik factory on the left and the new shopping mall on the right, which could provide essentials before cycling into the prosperous town of

Ehingen 492m (161/1206)
All facilities
This thriving town has much to see. There are several ancient churches all in good repair, a local history museum, many ancient timber-framed houses, an attractive market place and a fine town hall. (You could replenish supplies here if you did not visit the shopping mall passed earlier.)

Look for and follow the 'Blautal' signs (not obvious). Cycle in front of the railway station before turning sharp left to pass under the railway line then follow a narrow stream as the town is left behind.

The valley is initially wide with the cycleway swinging to the left away from the River Schmiech, but after passing through

Allmendingen 516m (167/1200)
Information, guesthouses, cycle shop, privately owned castle
the valley begins to narrow and display a distinctive limestone character.

Shortly the village of

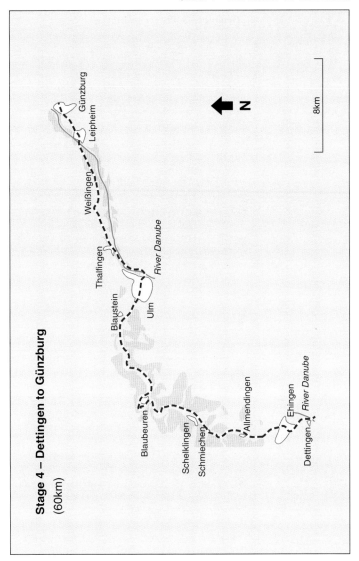

Stage 4 – Dettingen to Günzburg
(60km)

Schmiechen 530m (172/1195)
Information, guesthouses
is passed, and after crossing in front of the railway station the trail runs parallel to the railway line until it emerges in the attractive Bavarian town of

Schelklingen 529m (173/1194)
All facilities
The St Afra Chapel, Baroque church, ruined castle, picturesque market place with restored timber-framed houses and local history museums are all worth spending some time exploring.

On leaving the town, cross the railway and cycle on the right bank of the River Ach as it winds its way through a heavily wooded limestone gorge, with pinnacles of rock whose summits are often adorned with crosses or ruined castles visible on both sides. Having passed through the village of **Weiler** with its limestone caves the trail sweeps to the right before descending to the railway station on the edge of the town of

Blaubeuren 513m (181/1186)
All facilities
This busy tourist centre demands a lengthy stay if all its sights are to be visited and fully enjoyed. The Benedictine monastery is worth a lengthy visit. A chapel dedicated to St John was first constructed here in the eighth century and the monastery was founded in 1085 although not completed until 1510. Do not miss the cloisters, the garden and the beautiful St Peter's Chapel with its world-famous high altar.

The local history museum is also interesting but the famous Blautopf, close by, is extraordinary. Here water that looks forget-me-not blue, but is in fact clear, bubbles to the surface of a huge natural limestone cistern before flowing round the town as the River Blau. Alongside this pool is a water-driven blacksmith's shop where regular demonstrations are given. There are large numbers of tourists in high season.

From **Blaubeuren** to **Ulm** the Blau Valley begins to widen and the hills recede, providing easy, pleasant cycling with plenty of opportunities for picnics close to the river. A number of small villages and towns are passed including

Blaustein 491m (187/1180)
Information, hotel, guesthouses, rooms, cycle shop
Visits should be made to the pilgrim Church of Maria Hilf and to Klingenstein Castle.

The towns gradually merge to become suburban sprawl until the cycleway eventually leads into the centre of the city of

Ulm 468m (191/1176)
All facilities
This trading city was a thriving town as early as the twelfth century, most of its goods being transported in flat-bottomed barges along the Donau even as far as the Black Sea.

You will inevitably be led to the one landmark in Ulm which dominates all others, the tower of the minster, the highest church tower in the world. It is possible to climb to the viewing platform via a dizzying spiral staircase for stupendous views of the surrounding countryside. The minster itself is also worth visiting to see its modern stained glass including the Israelfenster, in memory of those killed in the Holocaust, the beautifully carved pulpit canopy and choir stalls, and the lavish church textiles housed under its soaring roof. Some of its older stained glass, which was removed for safety during the Second World War, has now been lovingly restored and replaced.

The vast square directly in front of it is often thronged with visitors but if it is quiet you can spend some time admiring the architecture of this ancient city with its fourteenth-century town hall cheek by jowl with the modern Stadthaus, which shocks many visitors. The town hall houses a fine astrological clock dating back to the sixteenth century. The architecture of the buildings that flank the square is exceptional.

Time can also be well spent losing yourself in the narrow medieval lanes and alleys that surround the square. The place abounds with museums of all kinds, one of the most interesting being the German Bread Museum, which is also a working museum, its main task being to research new strains of wheat to feed developing nations.

Ulm has at least two famous sons. One is Albert Einstein who is commemorated by an incredible fountain a kilometre away from the minster, a stone (*stein*) in the Health Administration Building and a monument on the spot of his birthplace. The second famous son was 'the tailor of Ulm', Albrecht Berblinger, who to all intents and purposes invented the hang-glider in an attempt to fly across the Donau from the city walls. The design worked although he failed in his attempt. A replica of his design can be seen in the Rathaus (town hall).

If in doubt about how to leave **Ulm** – there are few obvious signs – ask for directions down to the River Donau and, having reached it, turn left, following the riverside cycleway as it passes through a pleasant wooded linear park. This stretch can be crowded with other cyclists, parents with prams and the ubiquitous roller bladers! Although there is a cycleway on the opposite side of the river here it is advisable to keep to the left bank as far as

Thalfingen 465m (199/1168)
Information, hotel
There is little else of interest except the railway station.

The next section of the route may be surprisingly difficult to follow as sections of the riverside cycleway appear to have been closed. Instead of trying to follow it cycle alongside and along the main road, which is quite quiet, until the cycleway swings off to the right near the exit to a factory. Leave the main road here following the cycleway as it crosses the A7 motorway until it reaches

Weißingen 454m (206/1161)

No facilities

Here turn right off the paved way at an unlikely junction in the middle of the village (ask for Leipheim if you are unsure) onto an extremely rough and difficult length of trail, which is arrow straight for 4km, through a dense forest infested with voracious midges! Soon after it passes beneath the A8 motorway the track emerges from the trees to cross the Donau over a road bridge and, turning left, enters the busy little town of

Leipheim 450m (210/1157)

All facilities

This well-preserved and restored walled town has a historic centre with a fine fountain, castle, forteenth-century Parish Church of St Veit and local history museum.

There is no need to retrace your tracks over the Donau to regain the cycleway. Instead take the clearly signed, quiet but hilly road into

Günzburg 450m (218/1149)

All facilities

The superior youth hostel with restaurant (*Naturfreundehaus*) next to the campsite is reached by cycling out onto the far side of town (a long steep climb). The old town centre has been attractively restored and the Dominican church and local history museum can prove diverting.

STAGE 5
Günzburg to Altisheim (77km) – Total 295km

Leave **Günzburg** on the left bank of the river and follow the cycleway as it zigzags around field boundaries, undulating gently, passing through patches of broadleaf woodland after crossing the Donau. The river is not seen again until it is crossed after passing through

Offingen 434m (226/1141)
Information, rooms
If you have time visit the castle and the eighteenth-century Church of St Leonhard.

As soon as the Donau has been crossed the trail runs off at right-angles to it, crossing open flat lands with no sign of the river at all. There are no places of special interest but the cycling is easy and you pass through a string of small pretty towns.

Gundelfingen 433m (233/1134)
Information, hotel, guesthouses, rooms, cycle shop
Visit the Parish Church of St Martin, the town hall, the Schlachtegg Castle and the car museum.

Pass through the edge of the town (with the Donau nowhere in sight) and in a short time cycle into

Lauingen 435m (241/1126)
All facilities, cycle shop
See the classical architecture of the town hall and picturesque market square, the 'moldy' tower over 45m high, the castle, the minster and museums of local history and activities.

A long straight stretch of the cycleway leads into the larger, older town of

Stage 5 – Günzburg to Altisheim
(77km)

Altisheim

Donauwörth

Zusum

8km

Höchstadt

Steinheim

Dillingen

Lauingen

Gundelfingen

Offingen

Günzburg

N

Dillingen 425m (246/1121)
All facilities, cycle shop, campsite
There is a castle, a university with its own chapel and library, town hall, and several Baroque churches including the Parish Church of St Peter and the lavish early seventeenth-century Jesuit Studienkirche, which is worth seeing if only for the fantastic flights of fancy evident in its Baroque architecture.

From the town centre you can either follow the signs away from the river or drop down to it and follow the more picturesque left-bank cycleway until the two routes converge in the little village of

49

*Ancient gateway,
Dillingen*

Steinheim 426m (254/1113)
Information, guesthouse, cycle shop
No sooner have you left this village than the cycleway
leads into the town of

Höchstadt 418m (256/1111)
All facilities, campsite nearby
Places to visit include the Ducal Castle of the Pfalzgrafen
family from Pfalz-Neuburg, a fifteenth-century Baroque
parish church and a local history museum.

The **battle of Blenheim** took place in the village of Blenheim, just outside Höchstädt, on 13th August 1704. The battle marked the turning point in the War of Spanish Succession. Churchill, Duke of Marlborough, joined forces with Prince Eugene of Savoy to rout a Franco-Bavarian army commanded by Marshall Tallard and the Elector of Bavaria. It was a massive defeat for the French, the first in two generations, and it heralded the defeat of Bavaria and the saving of Vienna.

Having left **Höchstadt** be very careful to follow the signs as the cycleway turns sharp right in the village of **Blindheim**. It then crosses the Donau close to the village of **Gremheim** before wandering kilometres away from the right bank of the river across a patchwork of fields criss-crossed by many minor country roads until, at an unusual junction, the cycleway doubles back on itself. It then winds away at right-angles through a series of tiny hamlets and farmsteads. If the weather is inclement there is little shelter here except for an enormous yet beautiful beer-garden attached to a farm near Bäldleschwaige, shortly before entering the hamlet of

Zusum 401m (280/1087)
Rooms
Soon after the village the cycleway runs along the right bank of the Donau before crossing it and entering the striking Bavarian town of

Donauwörth 400m (282/1085)
All facilities, campsite
This is undoubtedly one of the most affluent towns in Bavaria with beautifully restored buildings and an air of pride in its heritage, no better expressed than in the fine main street with its brightly coloured houses and expensive, chic shops as well as its town hall, minster and churches. A long and productive time can be spent enjoying the architecture of this historic town with its step-gabled roofs, unexpected squares and tasteful sculpture. Climb the whole length of its main street to appreciate it fully.

Colourful gables in Donauwörth

Once Donauwörth has been thoroughly explored you need to descend back to the Donau but this time staying on its left bank. Soon the cycleway leaves the river, hugging the flanks of a number of steep hills to the left whilst undulating only gently itself. At this point the way runs alongside a busy road. Take care whenever the cycleway crosses from one side of the road to the other – which it does quite frequently!

Once the suburb of **Zirgesheim** has been passed the cycleway sweeps down towards the Donau but soon leaves it again as you enter the tiny attractive village of

Altisheim 450m (295/1072)
Guesthouse

STAGE 6

Altisheim to Landershofen (62km) – Total 357km

The trail leaves the Donau and heads towards the Altmühl Valley through spectacular limestone scenery. This stage of the cycleway provides three days of fascinating and picturesque cycling and manages to bypass some of the more industrial towns of the Donau Valley, such as Ingolstadt, before rejoining it at Kelheim.

From the outset, for the first time in days, the cycleway begins to undulate in a series of steep ascents and descents alongside the main road, which it crosses regularly (take care!). Occasionally the Donau is glimpsed meandering through woodland far below and to the right in its wide valley floor but the way is clearly signed through the small village of **Marxheim** and into the larger village of

Bertoldsheim 405m (308/1059)
Information, rooms, cycle shop
Time can be spent here visiting the fascinating eighteenth-century castle.

On leaving this small town turn left on a quiet leafy country road clearly signed to **Rennertshofen**. The Donau is now no longer in sight and will not be rejoined for another 120km. The road is still hilly as it climbs away from the river but soon reaches the outskirts of

Rennertshofen 392m (311/1056)
Hotel, bank, post office, campsite, cycle shop,
supermarket
On leaving the town follow the signs to **Hutting**. Now look for and follow large green and white signs saying *Altmühlradweg* (Altmühl – old mill, *Radweg* – cycleway). Many mills will be seen along the way, flanking the river, although few are still in use or working order.

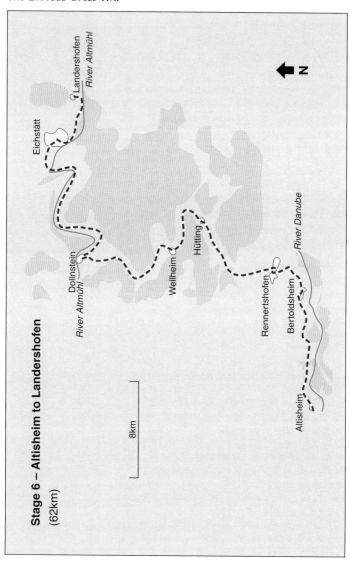

Stage 6 – Altisheim to Landershofen
(62km)

8km

The way begins with a slow easy climb along the flat bottom of a narrowing valley with woodland rising steeply on either side. The valley is considerably narrower than that of the Donau, which has recently been left, and arable farms abound on either side of the road with neat and well-maintained villages and farmsteads at regular intervals. The first sizable village to be cycled through is

Hutting (318/1049)
No facilities
Care should be taken in this area as there are a number of signs for the *Altmühlradweg* which lead unwary cyclists along rough awkward tracks only to deposit them, after a kilometre's toil, 100m further along the road they have just been cycling on! As the road itself is very quiet it is as easy to ignore the signs and stay on it, heading for

Wellheim (323/1044)
Hotel, bank, shelter
Continue through the valley, with steep woods on either side and excellent limestone scenery similar to that encountered on the first two days of the journey, only a little wilder. There are few communities along this stretch of the journey and it is 12km before the road finally leads into the busy little town of

Dollnstein (335/1032)
Information, post office, hotel, cycle shop
At this point you meet the River Altmühl, flowing down from the hills to the north. Here turn right onto the left bank of the Altmühl, which is clearly signed to **Eichstätt**. The river now swings in a series of wide meanders with steep wooded hills on each bank. Having cycled through **Breitenfurt**, keeping to the right bank of the river, cross the Altmühl twice more before embarking on a long right-hand bend with the castle of Willibaldsburg dominating the scenery high up to the right. Now keep to the well-signed bank of the river as it approaches and enters the university city of

Horse-drawn travel on the Altmühl Cycle Trail beyond Rennertshofen

Eichstätt (351/1016)

All facilities

The heart of this large ancient city can be reached by cycle track along the right bank of the Altmühl until a signed footbridge leads cyclists into the city centre.

The ancient market square, a favourite meeting place for those who attend Bavaria's largest Catholic university, with its large fountain flanked by well-preserved and interesting buildings, is surrounded by narrow cobbled medieval streets. The fifteenth-century minster with its soaring nave, stained-glass window by Hans Holbein the Elder and finely carved sandstone altar depicting a pilgrimage from Pappenheimer to Jerusalem is worth a lengthy visit. The Baroque reredos with gilded Germanic Virgin and the Diocesan Museum with many ecclesiastical pieces including twelfth-century artifacts on display should also be seen. If you have not yet had your fill of Baroque architecture the Jesuit Schutzengelkirche should satisfy your craving, as should the nearby ceiling of Notre Dame de Sacre Coeur.

Being a university town the central streets are often thronged with students although the high price of refreshments in the city centre does not reflect this. What is surprising is that most of the shops are closed on Saturday afternoons and the streets are consequently deserted. There is a sombre air to the city, unlike many of the other medieval university towns already visited. Large grey and cream stone houses are set alongside narrow medieval streets.

Return via the footbridge to the cycleway on the right bank of the river and follow it as it meanders through the suburbs of the city, which gradually become more agricultural until, after 5km, a village is reached – an ideal overnight halt if needed. Here cross the river and, having cycled at right-angles to it through the lower half of the village, cross the busy main road next to the large hotel to the upper half where, after climbing a steep hill, you reach

Landershofen (357/1010)
Hotel, rooms

STAGE 7
Landershofen to Dietfurt (50km) – Total 407km

The whole of this stage is through some of the most picturesque countryside Germany can offer.

Leave the village by turning left onto the main road and in a couple of kilometres turn left into the centre of the village of

Pfünz (361/1006)
No facilities
Follow signs to a spectacular reconstructed Roman fortress that stands high above the village. It is worth the short but steep climb to see it but it is advisable to leave your cycles at the bottom and tackle it on foot.

Return to the main road and cross both it and the river, following the well-signed cycleway on the left bank which leads through small farming communities. For the

Reconstructed Roman fort, Pfünz

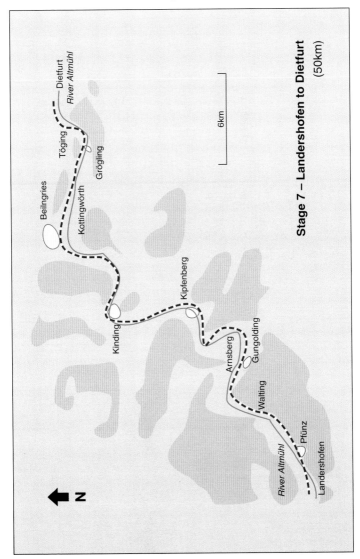

Stage 7 – Landershofen to Dietfurt

(50km)

6km

next 20km the route crosses and recrosses the river every kilometre or so, however there is little likelihood of getting lost as the way has prominent signs throughout.

Walting (366/1001)
Hotel, bank

After passing through the village the track surface alternates regularly between soft grit (difficult in both very dry and very wet weather) and smooth tarmac. As often in this area, quiet country lanes are 'bypassed' by long, poorly surfaced tracks that have a tendency to re-emerge onto the lanes, having provided nothing except muddy toil! If in doubt use the lanes with signposts to Gungolding.

The entry into

Gungolding (371/996)
Hotel

is heralded by a huge sweep of the river to the right. Soon afterwards the river swings left again in a great loop. Here, nestling below towering limestone cliffs, is the riverside town of

Arnsberg (374/993)
Hotel, bank

From here on the valley narrows and the cycleway keeps to the right bank of the river. Since the beginning of this stage of the route hardly a shop has been seen, so it may be with great relief that you approach the outskirts of

Kipfenberg (377/990)
Hotel, bank, guesthouses, rooms, shops

An imposing castle stands guard high above the town. If the weather is inclement there are seats and a simple shelter close to the shops.

The cycleway now runs close to the left bank of the river and is often sandy and occasionally rough. Care needs to be taken, especially in wet weather, as the track is often narrow and beset with overhanging branches and rampant vegetation. Pass under the Munich motorway and in a short time enter the village of

Kinding (385/982)
Hotel
Turn sharp right here (well signed) and keep to the left of the River Altmühl as it passes through the villages of **Pfraundorf** and **Badan-Hausen** before it leads into the beautiful Bavarian town of

Beilngries 367m (393/974)
All facilities, campsite, cycle shop on outskirts
This lovely old town deserves several hours of exploration. Its brightly coloured buildings are an architectural delight. Some have been restored but many are still in their original state of repair. An attractive town hall and an impressive church with twin spires decorated in multi-coloured tiles flank the cobbled town square.

Twin church spires, Beilngries

Its fine architecture and numerous souvenir shops and cafes tend to make the town a honeypot for tourists in high season and traffic in the town can be extremely heavy.

To exit Beilngries cross the river at the edge of the town and stay on its right bank. The scenery is similar to that seen during the earlier part of this stage of the cycleway except that the valley floor widens slightly here, although the sides are still steep. Where the trail meets the steep bank to the right of the river it turns sharp left, descending slightly until it reaches

Kottingwörth 365m (398/969)
Hotel, guesthouses, rooms
Do not miss the Church of St Vitus, if it is open. It has a series of very interesting frescos.

After following the right bank of the river closely as far as the village of

Grögling 366m (400/967)
Hotel
the trail now crosses the river, leaving it and passing through the centre of the small town of

Töging 368m (402/965)
Hotel
In a few more kilometres, after crossing both the old and new canals, you reach the outskirts of the bustling little town of

Dietfurt 364m (407/960)
All facilities
There is much to see here in this walled town including a fascinating museum of local life situated in the town's water mill and the historic market place with the Baroque Church of St Agidius. Several other churches here deserve a visit and there is a Franciscan monastery. The small motor museum has some unusual and interesting exhibits.

The town is famous for its strong and numerous connections with China (it is often referred to as the German Chinatown) although the origins of these connections seem unclear. There are displays about the links with China in several places including the town hall. At the end of July each year a big folk festival is held here that often features Chinese as well as local participants.

STAGE 8
Dietfurt to Weltenburg (40km) – Total 447km

The distance travelled on this stage is short to allow for the journey by boat along the Donau from Kelheim to Weltenburg and to allow plenty of time to explore the Bavarian riverside town and monastery of Weltenburg.

Leave **Dietfurt** by following the *Altmühlradweg* signs, making a long slow climb out of the town and keeping the tree-clad heights of Wolfsberg on your right. At the summit of the climb, against a fine backdrop of forests, will be found the picturesque little village of

Mühlbach 385m (410/957)
Information, hotel
Having left the village, sweep down a long hill towards the river and evidence of the Rhine-Main-Donau Canal. This undertaking has a very chequered history. The first canal proved to be an economic and practical disaster and the second, which many locals feel was never needed, appears to be suffering a similar fate. Keep them to the right until the cycleway reaches

Meihern 362m (414/953)
Information, guesthouses, rooms
Here join the riverbank near to the old and the new canals which have been constructed alongside the river and follow them as the River Altmühl widens and begins a series of huge meanders between steep tree-covered hills. There is little shelter hereabouts for cyclists if the weather is inclement and the wind has a tendency to be funnelled up the river valley.

Oberhofen 360m (420/947)
Guesthouse
is soon reached and passed as the river continues its wide meanders. After the dam at **Haidhof** the river swings to the left and passes through the town of

Riedenburg 361m (425/942)
All facilities, campsite
It is highly recommended that you cross the river to visit
the ancient quarter of this pleasant Bavarian town,

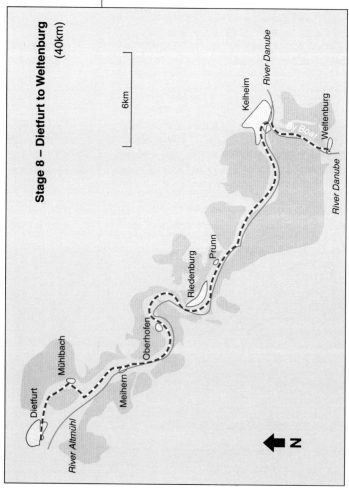

Stage 8 – Dietfurt to Weltenburg (40km)

6km

Dietfurt

Mühlbach

River Altmühl

Meihern

Oberhofen

Riedenburg

Prunn

Kelheim

River Danube

By Boat

Weltenburg

River Danube

N

famous for its falconry at the nearby Rosenburg Castle, where demonstrations are given daily, and for the Rhine-Main-Donau Canal on which you can sail.

The old quarter with its attractive town square has many tempting narrow streets and alleys, lined with antique shops, whilst the newer portion of the town has supermarkets to replenish supplies, and some of the most luxurious public toilets in Bavaria! There are a number of fine restaurants and cafes here serving large-portioned meals for hungry cyclists. One place that should certainly not be missed is the Crystal Museum, which contains many fascinating and priceless exhibits.

On leaving the town cross over the bridge to the left bank of the river and stay close to it in order to avoid a busy main road which sandwiches the cycleway between itself and the river. The beginning of the slope down to the track here is quite difficult to find (get off and walk if necessary) and care needs to be taken in order not to be sucked into the heavy traffic close to the bridge.

Within a couple of kilometres a huge castle towers above the trail to the left and dominates the scenery at the village of

Prunn 365m (429/938)

Guesthouses, rooms

The castle is built on a sheer pinnacle of Jurassic rock and was probably first constructed in the eleventh century. It can be visited between April and September and is note-worthy for its fine women's chamber and dungeon.

The rest of the cycling on this stage is along the left bank of the River Altmühl, close to but adequately separated by shrubs and trees from a very busy main road. The cycling is flat and easy with wooded hills rising on either side of the river until an increasing number of houses herald the approach to the city of

Kelheim 340m (439/928)

All facilities

See the monastery and the archaeological museum and, if you have the strength, climb up to see the Befreiungs-shalle (Liberation Hall) on the Michelsberg, which stands high on a hillside on the opposite bank of the river. King Ludwig I built it as a monument to remind people of the struggle against Napoleon and the need for all Germans to unite. To reach the huge iron doors you have to climb a steep flight of steps.

If you are not feeling so energetic a famous Bavarian brewery just off the fine ancient main square offers tours and tastings. The town can trace its origins back to the ninth century, its name meaning 'the town by the gorge'. The town gates and part of its ramparts can still be seen. It is from here to its mouth that the River Danube is truly navigable.

Cross the River Altmühl by the footbridge out of the modern section of the town into the old quarter. Pass through the gateway on cobbled streets and into the wide ancient main square of this traditional Bavarian town. The beautiful old buildings are worth examining in detail. Some have been restored but many are in their original state. Soon the River Donau will be seen once more. (If in doubt ask for the landing stages for the boats to Weltenburg.) Take the cycleway, which makes a hairpin bend down to the river, and with your cycle and most probably a host of other cyclists board a river-boat to **Weltenburg**.

There is no trail close to the river on this most spectacular section of the Donau so this 20-minute boat-trip is highly recommended to see the 'break-through' of the river. Here, with an amazing depth of 20m, the green waters of the Donau flow rapidly between high limestone cliffs often clothed in deciduous trees. The river here is very narrow and the water has sculpted the limestone into strange, beautiful shapes. In a short while disembark and cycle the few busy metres into the village of

Weltenburg 355m (447/920)
Information, hotels, guesthouses, rooms, brewery, restaurants, souvenir shops

See the great abbatial church here dated 1716 although the original monastery dates back to AD600. St Boniface converted the monastery into a Benedictine abbey in the eighth century and since then it has had a chequered history, losing its abbey status for a while before finally regaining it in 1913. Here, in the church dedicated to St Georg, can be seen Baroque decoration at its zenith. The gilded interior is quite incredible with fine frescos, brilliant statues and twisted marble pillars. If you have the energy and are prepared to leave your cycles unattended in the crowded main square, climb above the town to the charming little Frauenberg Chapel with its much more subdued decoration for spectacular views of the Donau. Beyond are the remains of a small Roman castle, presumably the origin of the town.

Descend via the Stations of the Cross into the busy cobbled town square to visit the brewery and sample the dark, rich beer from the oldest monastic brewery in the world, founded in 1058, and the souvenir shops. The 'real' modern town is beyond the monastery on the hill leading away from the river. Here can be found excellent food and accommodation at more reasonable prices than those demanded in the honeypot of the old town square.

Kloster Weltenburg from the Danube

STAGE 9

Weltenburg to Kirchroth (79km) – Total 526km

Climb quite steeply for several kilometres out of the town along the forested road which is clearly signed to **Kelheim**. The road is some distance from the river at this point and cannot be seen. A sharp descent brings you back into the city of Kelheim. Cross the river, taking great care in heavy traffic, and turn right. This junction is complicated and it may be necessary to dismount here to negotiate the traffic. Keep to the left bank of the Donau which for the first time is wide and deep enough to sustain fleets of barges operating on the river.

Ride out through the suburbs, keeping to the bank of the River Donau until you have passed

Kelheimwinzer 342m (451/916)
No facilities
The trail now climbs a little as it swings to the north of the Donau before descending to its banks once more a couple of kilometres short of

Poikam 338m (458/909)
Hotel, campsite
On leaving the town the trail makes a right-angle turn to the right, crossing a road and then the river onto a wide island in the Donau, heading for the town of **Bad Abbach**. Cross a second, very fine bridge to reach the far right bank and the outskirts of the town. Bad Abbach need not be entered; instead turn sharp left along the clearly signed cycleway beside the river and follow it as it rounds a steep spur of land with good views of the Donau. The cycling here is easy on a good fast surface and it is not long before the cycleway enters a public riverside park bustling with walkers, cyclists, roller-blade gymnasts and pram pushers. This continues for some time as the river swings to the right until the trail has passed a campsite and reaches the city of

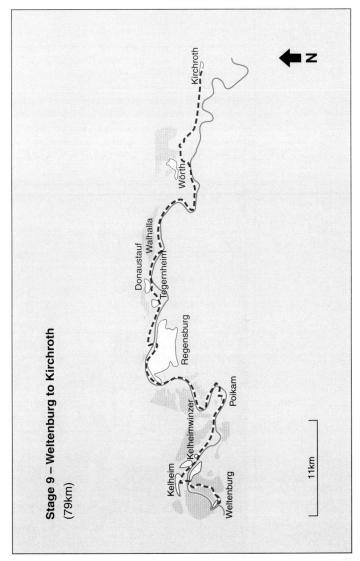

Stage 9 – Weltenburg to Kirchroth
(79km)

Regensburg 332m (478/889)
All facilities, campsite

This beautiful old city deserves considerable time being spent in it. Even Charlemagne visited it several times! The city centre alone contains over a thousand listed landmarks. There is a maze of narrow streets containing fine old houses, shops and museums, a lovely square with the magnificent twin-spired Dom St Peter, buildings with enormous painted frescos (David and Goliath is breathtaking) and an air of busy affluence. The Domschatz Museum has many church artifacts dating back to the tenth century.

The great Thurn and Taxis Castle that dominates the area close to the station can be visited to see the stronghold, the stables and the monastery, though the entry fee is very high for an obligatory guided tour.

David and Goliath mural, Regensburg

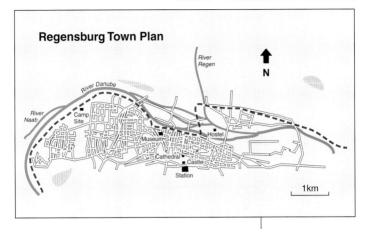

Regensburg Town Plan

The city once had a thriving Jewish community which has suffered terrible discriminatory attacks over the centuries. Memorials to these can be seen in several places throughout Regensburg and particularly in and around the Neupfarrplatz.

There are a large number of other sites and museums to visit in the city including the Historical, Imperial Diet, watch and Danube Navigation museums as well as the Kepler Tower with its beer-garden to the rear and the extensive Roman wall.

Last but by no means least, the cathedral dates back to the eighth century but has Carolingian, Ottonian and Gothic additions. Some of the stained glass surviving from as early as the thirteenth century is stunning, as are the statues to be found here including Regenburg's smiling angel giving Mary the good news of her pregnancy and the sinister Satan and Satan's grandmother. A walk around the beautiful cloisters and the crypt will complete a memorable visit.

The exit from the city needs care. A series of bridges leads across three islands in the Donau and its tributary, the River Regen. Follow the Frankenstraße through suburbs until the railway line is crossed and the cycleway swings beneath a main road onto the left bank of the Donau. The trail quickly leads to the edge of the small town of

Tegernheim 330m (487/880)
Hotel, guesthouse
The cycleway now leaves the river, skirting

Donaustauf 333m (491/876)
Information, hotels, guesthouses, rooms, cycle shop
If you have time see the pilgrim church of St Salvator near the exit to the town.

Less than a kilometre from the church, signs for 'Walhalla' appear on the far side of the main road that has been running parallel to the cycleway. This rather incongruous phenomenon should be visited if time allows. A steep woodland path leaving the left-hand side of the road climbs a hundred metres and leads to the foot of this massive neoclassical building, constructed in the mid-nineteenth century. Fully laden cycles should be wheeled some way up the slope rather than left exposed at the busy roadside.

Walhalla's steep, seemingly endless steps must be climbed if the view of the Danube plain stretching into

Walhalla, beyond Donaustauf

the Bavarian countryside from its portals is to be enjoyed. Care should be taken when approaching the main building as many people have been severely injured as a result of falls from its edges. You are warned not to cross the prominent white lines!

The building itself contains busts and memorials to Europe's greatest sons and daughters. Much discussion can be had here about who should or should not have been included (where are Shakespeare and Da Vinci and why are the only British commemorations to the Venerable Bede, King Egbert and St Boniface?). A diverting hour can easily be spent here if the clipboard-carrying school parties are not too overwhelming!

Return through the woods to collect your cycles and wheel them down to the cycleway, turning left onto it as the Donau Valley widens considerably. Although the cycling here is on the flat this stretch can be very tiring, particularly into a head wind, and there is very little shelter. Most of the towns and villages hereabouts are bypassed by the cycleway.

About 18km after leaving Walhalla, where the cycleway turns a right-angled bend to the left away from the Donau whose bank it has been hugging all the way, the town of

Wörth 322m (512/855)
Information, guesthouses, cycle shop
can be seen ahead on the far side of the A3 motorway, but the trail turns away from it to the right and leads alongside the motorway before wandering through arable farmland on rough tracks.

At the first proper paved road, turn right for **Stadldorf** and from there cycle through the attractive farming villages of **Niederachdorf**, **Pondorf** and **Oberzeitldorn**. Continue along the same road between fields of arable crops until you reach

Kirchroth 318m (526/841)
Post office, guesthouses

STAGE 10
Kirchroth to Passau (106km) – Total 632km

This final stage in Germany is quite a long ride. If you are planning to spend a night in Passau it is advisable to book your accommodation in advance as your destination is at the start of the most popular stretch of the Danube Cycle Way and Passau is always very busy with tourists, especially cyclists!

A pleasant, easy ride along flat roads leads through the hamlet of **Sossau** before the cycleway crosses the

Main square, Straubing

Donau via a series of islands that lead to a bridge into the 'Secret Seat of Government of Bavaria',

Straubing 318m (536/831)
All facilities, campsite
This is a beautiful old city with a fine square at its centre where a graceful tower, the Stadtturm, stands over 60m above the square which it bisects. Alongside it stands the fourteenth-century Rathaus (town hall) which has been much restored. The sun-emblazoned Trinity Column can also be found here. The buildings around the square are outstanding not only for their architectural style but also for the intensity of their bright colours.

The ancient quarter of Straubing lies between the Donau and the railway station. There are several churches demanding a visit including the Romanesque Basilica of St Peter, the Church of St James and the Carmelite and the Ursuline churches. The nearby Gäuboden Museum houses one of the richest collections of Roman artifacts in Germany.

In August the town hosts one of the greatest beer festivals in Europe when up to a million visitors descend upon the town: 23,000 seats fill the main square and this and all the side streets are filled with devotees of Bavaria's finest brews. At this time accommodation here is almost impossible to find.

The exit from the city is not easy to find. Recross the bridge which led into the town and turn immediately right onto the cycleway before crossing the Agnes Burnauer Bridge and turning sharp right again, following the riverbank. After several kilometres of cycling across flat farmland the trail runs into

Bogen 390m (544/823)
All facilities
Try to spend some time in the pilgrim church and visit the local history museum as well as the castle for the splendid views.

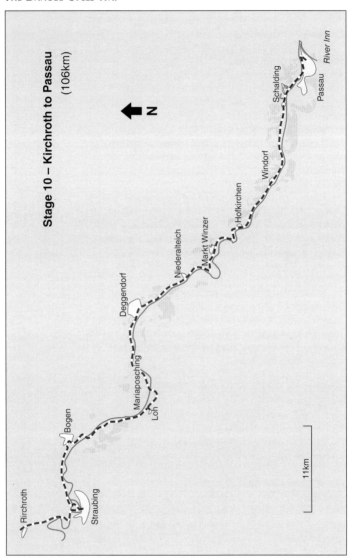

Stage 10 – Kirchroth to Passau
(106km)

N

Rirchroth

Bogen

Straubing

Mariaposching

Loh

Deggendorf

Niederalteich

Markt Winzer

Hofkirchen

Windorf

Schalding

Passau

River Inn

11km

As soon as the town has been left behind take a right turn to cross the Donau and turn left to take roads through arable farmland. Pass through the hamlets of **Entau** and **Irlbach** before following signs in the village of **Wischlburg**, away from the signed cycleway, to visit the famous masterpiece of Baroque church architecture at

Loh 315m (557/810)
No facilities
The Church of the Holy Cross should not be missed. Its exterior is quite simple but its interior takes your breath away. It is extravagantly decorated in the Baroque style like some vast Christmas cake with pink and white plasterwork rising to the painted ceiling in tiers. The whole edifice is dripping with gold.

Regain the cycleway at Wischlburg and cycle on into the straggling town of **Stephansposching** before turning left at the sign to the simple car ferry across the Donau into

Mariaposching 313m (561/806)
No facilities
Turn right onto the trail which closely follows the left bank of the river. This is a pleasant if unexciting stretch of the route which facilitates visits to villages, if necessary, but does not pass through the centre of any community until the cycleway enters

Deggendorf 315m (571/796)
All facilities, campsite
There are a number of churches worth visiting here including that dedicated to Saints Peter and Paul as well as the town hall with its tower plus a couple of local museums dedicated to crafts and boat-building.

On leaving the city take the cycleway which travels alongside the motorway for a while before the trail makes a climbing hairpin to cross it, thereafter hugging the river-bank. There is water to be seen everywhere here as the

River Donau widens and numerous lakes are formed. Cycle alongside the river until the cycleway enters

Niederalteich 312m (580/787)
Information, hotels, guesthouses, rooms
If there is time try to visit both the Benedictine abbey and the basilica.

Do not cross the river by the ferry here but follow the track alongside the Donau until a country lane which is not clearly signed leaves to the left in the direction of a town and castle just discernible on the skyline. Take this and, after passing under the motorway, cycle into

Markt Winzer 311m (590/777)
Information, guesthouses, rooms, cycle shop
The ruined castle is well worth a visit for the views of the Donau Valley.

The cycling here is flat and easy, sometimes on the river-bank, at others cutting the corners of meanders but never far away from the Donau which can usually be seen.

Hofkirchen 305m (598/769)
Information, guesthouses, rooms
is quickly passed and soon afterwards the trail clings to the riverbank while pleasant woodlands appear to the left. Soon the city of **Vilshofen** can be spied on the far bank and a small airfield and runway can be seen separating the cycleway from the riverbank.

The scenery now improves and is fairly similar to that of the English Lake District. The trail too begins to undulate, although it is nothing that a simple gear change can't handle!

Windorf 301m (613/754)
Information, hotel, guesthouses, cycle shop
is soon passed as the scenery constantly improves, with forested hills now appearing on both sides of the valley. Stay on the left bank of the Donau as the cycleway stays

close to it until, in the distance, the first signs of the end of this stretch appear. By the time the cycleway has reached

Schalding 308m (625/742)
Guesthouse, rooms

the suburbs of Passau are evident on the far bank of the river but this is a very large city and there is still far to go. At the suburb of Maierhof cross the road beside which you have been cycling and follow the rather confusing signs, taking the bridge over the Donau, and turn left to ride into the city. As soon as possible keep close to the right bank of the river and, if all the signs are followed diligently, this will lead to the city centre.

Passau 300m (632/735)
All facilities, campsite

There is enough to see and do here to justify spending a whole day or two in the city. It is built at the confluence of three rivers: the Ilz, a minor tributary, the Donau, which you have been following, and the Inn, by far the largest of the three, which now gives up its name to the new and mighty Donau. Viewed from the heights of the

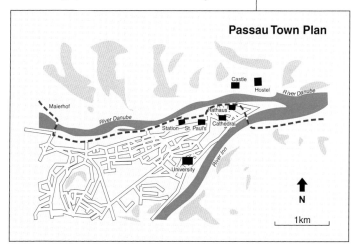

Confluence of the rivers Inn and Danube, Passau

Veste Oberhaus Castle the confluence is quite strange as the two larger rivers have entirely different hues: the Inn is the colour of jade whilst the Donau is muddy brown. It is a few miles downstream before the new river assumes its overall brown colour.

The old part of the city is a delight. A broad promenade leads to the town hall with its astounding carillon. This was once Passau's fish market, and the high-water marks carved into the building indicate the destructive power of the river when it is in full flood. Visit the interior of the town hall with its lavish state assembly rooms painted extravagantly by local artists.

From here a cobweb of narrow alleys winds up towards the Domplatz in front of the great Cathedral of St Stephan. This massive church was originally constructed in 997 but has been rebuilt several times since then. It claims to be the largest Baroque building north of the Alps and houses the largest church organ in the world. This is in reality five organs strategically placed throughout the cathedral linked to a single manual. (Daily concerts are

The great organ in the Dom St Stephan, Passau

81

given at 12 noon but huge queues form long before the start of each concert – doors open at 11.20am.)

As in so many of the great churches along the route the walls and ceilings are covered in ornate frescos, stucco and fanciful gilding epitomised by the great golden eighteenth-century pulpit. One of the most moving parts of the cathedral is the modern high altar with its depiction of the stoning of its patron saint, St Stephan.

The other religious building not to be missed is the Parish Church of St Paul. This Baroque church stands on the site of earlier Romanesque and Gothic buildings. Unlike the cathedral there is little in the way of frescos or stucco work here. Instead great black and gold altars, organ and pulpit dominate the interior, giving a very different impression of Baroque adornment.

The Veste Oberhaus over a hundred metres above the city is worth the long climb if only for the panoramic views from the top. To reach it cross the Luitpoldbrücke suspension bridge and climb the path to the top of the hill before you. Although the building is almost 800 years old it has a curiously modern air about it, and it is no surprise to find a panoramic restaurant offering the finest views of Passau along with local delicacies. It also houses the extensive local Cultural History Museum.

The glass museum is breathtakingly large with 35 rooms on four floors housing over 30,000 exhibits. There is so much to see that a considerable amount of your time could easily be spent in here. Other museums include the Shipping and Salt Trade Museum, the Treasury and Diocesan Museum, the Roman Museum and the Museum of Modern Art. If you are not interested in any of these a stroll through the Hals district on either side of the River Ilz will lift your spirits.

A number of churches are worth visiting including the pilgrimage church that stands high above the town on the south bank.

STAGE 11
Passau to Linz (100km) – Total 732km

If you now feel like making progress without having to pedal, the cruise ships that ply their trade up and down the Danube make an interesting alternative. The journey from Passau to Linz can be made on one of these boats in a single day, passing through magnificent scenery with the added interest of passing through a number of gigantic locks where hydroelectric power stations straddle the Danube. The boats are comfortable with plenty of room for cycles and they provide refreshments and meals.

However, if you are a purist, it is time to climb back into the saddle! For most of the rest of the journey the cycleway runs on both banks of the river. At times there is little to choose between the two routes, but if one is more attractive than the other it has been described here. You will also notice that between here and Vienna the quality of the trail is excellent. There are some short stretches on cycle lanes alongside roads but the majority of the trail is now on dedicated, smooth, paved, traffic-free cycleways. From here onwards you will find *Radstationen* (information bureaux especially for cyclists on the Donau trail – see Introduction) at regular intervals along the way.

Take the southern route out of Passau by crossing the River Inn and turn left, following signs which keep you close to the right bank of the river. Cycle alongside and occasionally on the road through the now empty customs office between Germany and Austria. Some of the cycleway from here is away from the road and some follows it. Cycle through the hamlet of **Parz** where accommodation is available and on past the **Faberhof Inn** until the cycleway leads into

Pyrawang 295m (645/722)
Information, rooms, campsite
Spend some time admiring the Gothic frescos in the parish church.

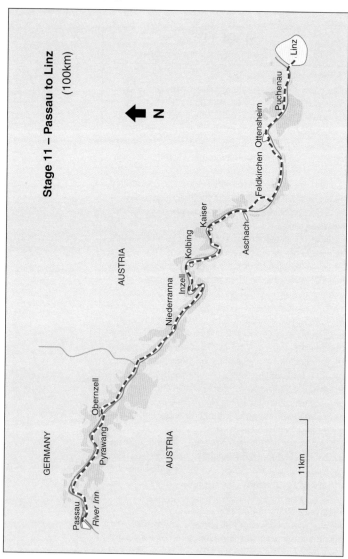

Stage 11 – Passau to Linz
(100km)

N

GERMANY

AUSTRIA

Passau
River Inn
Pyrawang
Obernzell
Niederranna
Inzell
Kolbing
Kaiser
Aschach
Feldkirchen
Ottensheim
Puchenau
Linz

AUSTRIA

11km

Ride through the village, continuing to follow the trail signs, until the car ferry across the Donau is reached in 3km. Cross this to

Obernzell 293m (648/719)
Information, hotel, guesthouses, rooms
This town was once famous for its pottery and there is a pottery museum at the castle with examples from the Neolithic era to the present. The market square houses a fine rococo church and a beautifully decorated inn depicting the production of wine for which the town was once famous.

The cycleway now undulates as it follows the left bank of the Donau although the fine scenery will quickly distract you from the extra effort needed on this stretch. Cycle past the hydroelectric power station and locks at **Jochenstein** keeping to the cycleway as it runs parallel to the left bank. Soon the small town of **Engelhartszell** with its Trappist monastery can be seen on the other side of the river. If you wish to visit this a ferry is available. If not stay on the left bank and in a kilometre a *Radstation* will offer help and snacks. The scenery becomes increasingly impressive as the cycleway heads into the village of

Niederranna 289m (664/703)
Information, guesthouses, rooms, campsite
The 700-year-old castle has nothing of particular interest.

Turn right under the bridge and follow the trail as the valley undulates and narrows. Soon the River Danube's great 180-degree meander is reached and a choice awaits you. There are three cyclists' ferries here (if they are all running). One takes you directly across the Donau to **Schlögen** (unnecessary unless you have some pressing need to visit the hotel or the cycle repair shop). A second leaves the trail a few hundred metres further on at a farmhouse selling local produce. This makes a short direct crossing of the river. A third, infrequent and unreliable service sails 3–4km downstream to deposit you at Grafenau, which is on the wrong side of the river. The second option seems the most sensible and reliable, and from the right bank just beyond the ferry landing stage the views of the great meander are spectacular. The route then leaves the riverbank for a short while until it arrives in

Inzell 285m (676/691)

Information, guesthouse, rooms, campsite
Go and see St Nicholas's Church which is said to have been built in thanks by a nobleman after he was saved from drowning.

As the river meanders fresh vistas appear every minute. Soon the attractive village of **Obermühl** with its ancient seventeenth-century capped silo, once a customs office, appears on the far bank. This can be reached by ferry from

Kolbing 285m (681/686)

Information, no facilities
This stretch of the river teems with wildlife and it is not unusual to see deer, otters and polecats crossing the trail together with numerous birds of prey circling overhead. After another series of meanders the trail, which is still on the right bank, reaches

Kaiser 280m (692/675)

Hotel, campsite
A ferry connects **Untermühl**, on the opposite bank, and if you wish to visit the famous chain tower of Neuhaus Castle, one of the great castles of Upper Austria, this is the way to do it. Otherwise continue on the right bank along a remarkably straight stretch of the river after so many meanders until the next dam (with *Radstation*) is passed and you cycle onto the fine promenade of

Aschach 276m (700/667)

All facilities
The town centre is worth visiting with its old stucco-adorned houses and seventeenth-century ruined castle.

The parish church is fifteenth century but the Hartkirchen church is reputed to have been founded in the ninth century and contains wall and ceiling frescos with a *trompe l'oeil* element making the whole church seem bigger. The town's fortune has always been associated with the river (it was originally a toll station) and shipbuilding still has a part to play in Aschach's life. The fine promenade along which the cycleway runs is lined with fine brightly coloured buildings.

Cross the Donau Bridge with care and watch out for a signed track to the right immediately after the bridge. This path leads through suburbs and sweeps away from the river through affluent farmsteads until it reaches

Feldkirchen 268m (705/662)
Information, guesthouses, rooms, campsite, leisure park with water sports
An interesting sixteenth-century parish church.

At the crossroads in the centre of town take the track to the right to regain the Donau's left bank in a couple of kilometres. The trail now follows the raised bank of the river until the next dam is in sight. Here turn sharp left and follow a branch of the Donau. Soon it is apparent that this water has been marked off for rowing races. At the boat club turn left and follow the signs on a tortuous stretch of the cycleway until it leads into the centre of

Ottensheim 270m (719/648)
All facilities, campsite, cycle shop
The town square of this bustling market town has many attractive houses including the Kindlhaus. The castle keep and fifteenth-century parish church containing skeletons and a mummified woman should be seen although the former cannot be visited.

The exit from the town is complicated but not difficult if the signs are followed. Having crossed the railway keep it on your right for the 6km into

Puchenau 266m (726/641)

Rooms (to the left above the village), shops and supermarket (alongside the road), railway (right of the traffic lights)

The route is obvious now as it runs parallel to the river and the railway, passing beneath the latter before running along narrow one-way streets as it approaches the bridge into the centre of

Linz 256m (732/635)

All facilities, campsite

This is another city that demands time spent in it. One day is hardly enough. Renowned for its steel-making prowess, its chemical factories and the fact that Hitler intended it as the capital of his empire, you are not prepared for the elegance and sheer beauty of this place. It sits astride the Donau with its old quarter on the South Bank. Fine Baroque buildings surround one of the most picturesque squares in Austria, the Hauptplatz. The square also houses the Dreifaltigkeitssäule (Trinity Column), a 20m marble

Hauptplatz, Linz

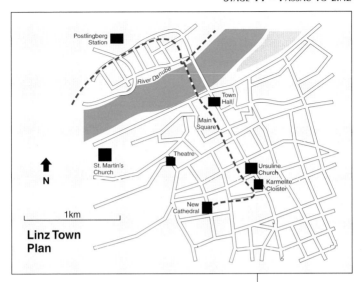

Linz Town Plan

Baroque column announcing the gratitude of the guilds, emperor and people of Linz for deliverance from war, fire and the plague.

The spire of the neo-Gothic New Cathedral, which can seat 20,000 people, with its brightly coloured painted glass, towers over the city yet only a few minutes' walk away is the tiny eighth-century gem of St Martin's Church, built partly out of Roman stones. Inside the church Roman stone inscriptions and a furnace can be seen. These are only two of many fascinating ecclesiastical buildings which include the seventeenth-century Karmeliterkirche, the eighteenth-century Ursulinenkirche, the Seminarkirche built for the Order of German Knights, and the old cathedral built in the second half of the seventeenth century. It was here that Anton Bruckner served as cathedral organist.

One of the most interesting churches is the Pöstlingberg, reached by the steepest non-rack railway in the world, and from which magnificent views can be had in all directions. If possible climb to the summit on the railway but descend on foot as the views of Linz as you descend are remarkable. The Landhaus, which began life as a Renaissance monastery, is now the seat of provincial government. It is worth walking through its arcaded interior and fountain-filled courtyards just to absorb its atmosphere.

There is enough fine architecture and museums to fill a couple of days easily. If you are tired, relax in one of the shady parks, eat and drink in the restaurants and bars which abound, or spend an hour watching the outdoor chess-players perform mental calisthenics near the Trinity Column.

STAGE 12

Linz to Grein (78km) – Total 810km

To leave the city, cross the bridge back onto the left bank and turn right through parkland close to the Donau passing beneath a railway and then a road bridge. This is the area in which many of Linz's citizens take their daily exercise so watch out for other cyclists, joggers and hundreds of people on roller blades who swoop and dive around unwary cyclists at dizzying speeds. The way is clearly signed as it skirts a campsite and lake much favoured in fine weather by naturists. On the far bank of the river are huge iron, steel and chemical works belching smoke and steam but on the left bank the scenery is already rural. There is no need to turn off the track to visit **Steyregg** unless you would like to see the frescos in St Stephen's Church or the dominant thirteenth-century castle. Otherwise cycle on along the bank, taking special care at a 'kink' in the route near a yachting marina until, a kilometre short of the Abwinden-Asten Dam, a cyclists' shelter will be found. Turn sharp left here and pass close to the railway line at **Abwinden-Gusen Station** before turning right, avoiding St Georgen but heading along badly signed, confusing roads lined with bungalows towards **Gusen**, famous for its primeval hilltop settlement just to the south. The cycleway appears to be in the process of being changed in this area, with doubtful or nonexistent signs, and it is advisable, if in doubt, to ask for directions to

Langenstein 245m (754/613)
Information, rooms, bar
Cycle through well-tended suburbs parallel but away from and out of sight of the river and major road that runs alongside it. On a right-hand bend, having descended a short hill, you will pass a sign to the former concentration camp 2km to the left of the trail. At this sombre reminder of Germany's past over 120,000 people who were made

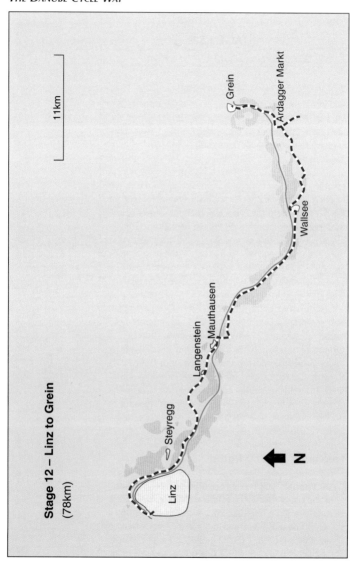

Stage 12 – Linz to Grein
(78km)

11km

N

Grein
Ardagger Markt
Wallsee
Mauthausen
Langenstein
Steyregg
Linz

to quarry granite nearby were put to death between 1939 and 1945. Finally enter the picturesque thirteenth-century town of

Mauthausen 244m (758/609)
All facilities, cycle shop, campsite nearby

The town's prosperity has grown from tolls it has extracted over the years from mariners. See the Gothic Church of St Nicholas and, by the river, a beautiful row of seventeenth-century houses with striking murals. The most outstanding of these is the Chalet Wedi with pargeter work depicting strange scenes of life in ancient Mauthausen including what appears to be a dentist's surgery fully equipped with gruesome instruments! The prettiness of this riverside town is in stark contrast to its grizzly recent past witnessed at the site of the concentration camp.

Decorated houses in Mauthausen

From Mauthausen it is possible to cycle on either side of the river. The left bank track is smooth and lined with a complex of large supermarkets if they are required. The right bank is rough in places but has much to delight both the eye and the palate!

Ignore the road to Enns unless you want to visit the town's city tower and Basilika St Laurenz. Otherwise take the bridge alongside the railway (not the ferry) to cross the Donau, and in **Pyburg** turn left at the station, crossing a narrow tributary before regaining the right bank of the Donau. Do NOT take the track to the right in a couple of kilometres (clearly signed 'St Pantaleon') but persist on the *Treppelweg* (old towpath). This can sometimes be flooded but if not follow it as it skirts the fluvial forest of poplar (linden) trees – Austria's national emblem. For a couple of kilometres the track is rough but the tarmac is soon regained and after 5–6km the official cycleway rejoins the *Treppelweg* from the right. With the castle of **Wallsee** already in sight, pass alongside the dam of **Wallsee-Mitterkirchen** (do not cross it). Soon afterwards cross a tributary of the Donau and in no time you will find yourself at the impressive hilltop town of

Wallsee 231m (779/588)

Information, guesthouses, rooms, campsite
The great sixteenth-century castle with its 70m keep dominates the town. To the south of the town but worth visiting is the Gothic parish church at Sindeburg with Baroque decoration.

For 12km or so the trail now passes through a very different landscape, the Mostviertel, given over to the cultivation of apples and pears to make the famous local drink *most* – a strong, still cider. You may be tempted by numerous hostelries along the way to sample it but be warned! It is just as strong as English 'scrumpy' and sold in bigger glasses! This section of the route is several kilometres away from the river which is not seen again until a kilometre after reaching the sprawling town of

Ardagger Markt 245m (792/575)

Information, hotel, guesthouses, rooms, cycle shop
The town has museums of the army, farming and the manufacture of *most*.

An excursion (turn right) to the former abbey church (5km round trip including a short climb) is worth the effort. It has an eleventh-century Romanesque crypt and, in the St Margaret window, claims to have the oldest painted glass in Austria. The Mostgalerie in front of the abbey serves *most* and other related products.

On returning to Ardagger Markt cycle straight on through the town, parallel with the main road before crossing it and cycling through an attractive little backwater. In a couple of kilometres the cycleway eventually leads back onto the right bank of the Donau. Follow this to the next bridge (signed to 'Grein') and take great care crossing it as the traffic here is often fast and heavy. Then return under the bridge to cycle a narrow riverside track on the left bank which soon leads into the beautiful ancient town of

Grein from the opposite bank of the Danube

Grein 230m (810/557)
All facilities, cycle shop, campsite
This most attractive of Danubian towns is dominated by the seventeenth-century Greinburg Castle with its fine arcaded courtyard, and boasts a comprehensive shipping museum, an attractive sixteenth-century town hall, the oldest municipal theatre (built in 1790) in the country and some architecturally stunning buildings including the late Gothic St Agidius' Church. This is the 'romantic' Danube town you have been searching for!

95

STAGE 13
Grein to St Michael (77km) – Total 887km

Unfortunately the first 2km of this stretch is a retracing of the route as far as the bridge over the Donau. Once again cross it with great care and turn to cycle back along the opposite bank. This junction is confusing. If in doubt get off and walk, following signs. Remember that you should be cycling towards Grein again but this time on the opposite bank of the river. The scenery hereabouts is breathtaking, probably the most beautiful encountered anywhere on the journey. Tree-clad mountains rise on both sides of the river and tiny villages nestle by the water's edge.

The river has a reputation beyond Grein for dangerous currents, its narrowness, whirlpools and even pirates! As you pass the imposing villages of **Struden** and **St Nikola** on the opposite bank it is easy to believe. At one time the rocky riverbed caused so many accidents that this stretch of the river was known as 'the place where death resides'. Fortunately the reefs have now been blasted away and river traffic can negotiate the bend in safety.

After cycling past the old toll station of Werfenstein Castle on the far bank, the river widens slightly, though the scenery is no less beautiful. Soon you will reach

Freyenstein 231m (826/541)
No facilities, guesthouse
An impressive ruined castle dominates the village. Freyenstein is a pretty village famous in local folklore as the home of Nöck, the Lord of the Danube.

In a short time the cycleway runs into

Willersbach 229m (828/539)
Inn, campsite
At the power station and dam which soon appear the river can be crossed in order to visit **Persenbeug** with its

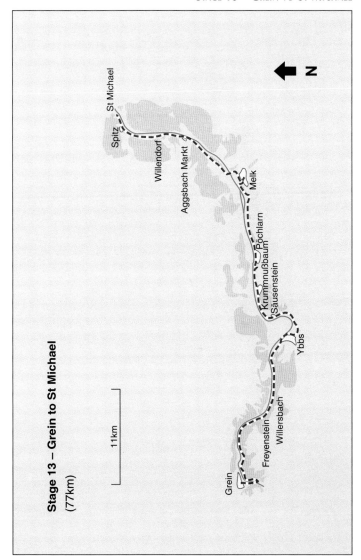

mighty Habsburg castle, birthplace of Emperor Karl I, and huge Gothic Church of St Florian, outside which stands a 700-year-old lime tree. Otherwise simply cycle past the *Radstation* and follow the promenade on the right bank of the river into the pretty little town of

Ybbs 222m (839/528)

Information, hotel, guesthouses, rooms, campsite, cycle shop

In the past Ybbs has suffered from fires and floods but this picturesque old town with its moat still in existence is worth exploring. There are beautifully restored houses with shady vine-covered courtyards surrounding the old market square, and the fifteenth-century St Lawrence's Church has much to commend it including a fine high altar and organ. It also boasts a strange depiction of the Mount of Olives complete with fourteenth-century figures moulded from clay. There is an interesting cycle museum a short distance from the church with some sculptures made from cycle parts.

The transition from the old quarter to the new part of the town is startlingly abrupt. The exit from the town can be confusing. If possible follow the cycleway signs for 'Melk'. The trail swings erratically crossing the River Ybbs, passing through allotments, industrial premises and a wood-yard before emerging again on the right bank of the Donau after a surprisingly long time.

The track now follows the river and railway through fluvial forest passing the village of

Säusenstein 226m (844/523)

Rooms

See the remains of a fourteenth-century chapel and the Baroque Church of St Donatus high above the village.

The trail now runs alongside the newly built high-speed railway which tends to dominate the scene until the cycleway passes through the edge of

Krummnussbaum 219m (849/518)

Guesthouses, rooms

This market town has an eleventh-century castle, the wooden fourteenth-century Church of St Nicholas and a village chapel dated 1803.

Here the trail exactly follows the right bank of the river. This stretch is long and exposed and can be tiresome if the wind is strong and not behind you. Soon after a tight hairpin to negotiate an inlet via a bridge (take care with traffic here) enter the town of

Pöchlarn 213m (855/512)

Information, hotel, guesthouses, rooms, campsite, cycle shop

Here there are art galleries, a rebuilt fourteenth-century Gothic church with reused Roman tombstones in its wall (this was the site of the Roman town Arelape) and the defensive Welser Tower which is now a local museum. A new bridge over the Donau was built in 2000. The hill-top monastery containing the treasures of Melk can now be seen in the distance ahead.

The river's edge is followed until the Neuwinden Dam is sighted but at this point the trail turns away from the river, past a *Radstation*, before regaining the bank for just over a kilometre. The trail once again swings sharp right and passes a coach park before crossing the River Melk and the main road (very busy junction – take great care) as it leads into the centre of the busy little tourist town of

Melk 213m (865/502)

All facilities, youth hostel, campsite, cycle shop

For several kilometres the great monastery at Melk has dominated the skyline and now it towers above the town, unassailable by cycles which have to be left in the town square if you wish to take a tour of the monastery.

The town has thrived since the year 976 when the Babenbergs took up residence here. The great Bene-dictine monastery, one of Europe's most splendid

Benedictine Abbey, Melk

Baroque structures with its mass of treasures, is certainly worth a visit. The Imperial Chambers of the monastery are now used as a museum area where exhibitions show Melk's historic and artistic importance. The Abbey Church of St Peter and St Paul, which was restored and regilded in 1998, is full of Baroque splendour, described as 'a symphony of colour and form'. The church contains a famous organ built to replace the one damaged in 1929 and a fine marble altar was installed as recently as 1976. The world-famous library with its eighteenth-century ceiling frescos should not be missed. It contains over 100,000 volumes and manuscripts dating back to the ninth century.

The ancient and restored town square is very attractive but can often be very crowded with tourists. The best way to see the old town is to acquire a town map from the local tourist office as this has a worthwhile suggested itinerary taking in the most important sights.

Leaving Melk is both navigationally tricky and physically hard work! Return to the main road and turn right onto the cycle track to the left of the road (beware of heavy traffic). At the Y-junction take the right fork which climbs steeply and steadily high above the river. Then take the second road to the left which leads down over the Donau bridge. Follow the loop downwards until it reaches the main road on the left bank of the river almost opposite a *Radstation* and turn left onto the cycleway which follows the left bank towards Krems.

Some sections of the cycleway now run alongside a busy main road and the trail is often very narrow and can be overgrown. This continues most of the way to

Aggsbach Markt 214m (877/490)
Information, guesthouses, rooms
Situated at the foot of the Jauerling (957m), the village boasts a thirteenth-century Romanesque parish church. Mammoth hunters in the Ice Age first settled here and there is a museum of the Stone Age.

Now you are entering the Wachau, centrepiece of the great Germanic medieval epic poem *Nibelungenlied*, extracts of which can be seen in a 700-year-old version in Melk. This is undoubtedly one of the most pleasant stretches of the entire route. For the first time since leaving Donaueschingen, vineyards appear in abundance accompanied by peach, plum and apricot orchards. Vine-clad mountains appear on both sides of the river and there is a general atmosphere of wellbeing inherent in the whole region, which has a mild 'soft' climate.

Now the trail stays close to the local railway line but often leaves the main road to wander through the wine-producing villages, almost all of which offer accommodation of one sort or another.

Willendorf 209m (880/487)
Information, rooms
This is the site of a Stone Age settlement. In 1908 a tiny (11cm) statue of a woman (the Willendorf Venus) was found here and is accepted as being the most beautiful Paleolithic figure ever found. Large copies of the statue are to be found along the way, as is a museum of the Stone Age.

Venus of Willendorf

After wandering through the lower slopes of the vineyards, past apricot trees and through villages of golden stone, one of the major Wachau villages is reached,

Spitz 223m (885/482)
Information, hotels, guesthouses, rooms, cycle shop

In good years this town, which dates from 865, produces in the region of 56,000 litres of wine. The great Erlauhof Castle and the ruined castle of Hinterhaus dominate the town. It is worth entering the triple-aisled Church of St Mauritius in the market place to see its Gothic interior, net vaulting and Baroque high altar. The old town hall and hospital surround a picturesque courtyard whilst the Red Gate provides an opportunity for photographers and artists to practise their skills.

Follow the cycle trail signs for Krems and cycle out of the village with the railway and the river on your right. Soon cross over the railway and cycle through the finest vineyards in the Wachau to the wine village of

St Michael 211m (887/480)
Information, rooms, restaurant, bar

Excellent food and wine can be had from Weinstubes, decorated with garlands, in the village. The fifteenth-century church was the focal point for the first parish in the Wachau. Look for the hares on the presbytery roof.

STAGE 14

St Michael to Langenlebarn (84km) – Total 971km

Continue cycling through idyllic countryside into the famous wine town of

Weissenkirchen 224m (892/475)

Information, hotels, guesthouses, rooms

The fourteenth-century church, reached by a covered walkway, is half ecclesiastical building, half fortification. It is worth walking around its outside as well as its interior. The market place has a fine arcaded fifteenth- century courtyard which is the site of the Lower Austrian Wine academy. The Wachau and Winegrowers' museum should certainly be visited. Try a stroll along the picturesque promenade, especially in the evening as the gold of the dying sun is reflected a million times in the fast-flowing Danube.

Cycle out of the town over the level crossing and enter the Frauengärten where small buildings can be seen dotted among the vineyards. The valley becomes enclosed once more by mountains, and soon after, the imposing castle of Dürnstein, in which Richard Coeur de Lion is said to have been imprisoned, comes into view, heralding the entrance to the busy town of

Dürnstein 226m (898/469)

Information, hotels, guesthouse, rooms

The town is often full of visitors on day trips from Vienna. They come to see the castle where Richard the Lion Heart was held prisoner and the brightly coloured Augustinian abbey and its courtyard, both on a much smaller scale than those at Melk. This is one of the Wachau wine centres, and tastings take place at the nearby Baroque Kellerschlößl wine cellar.

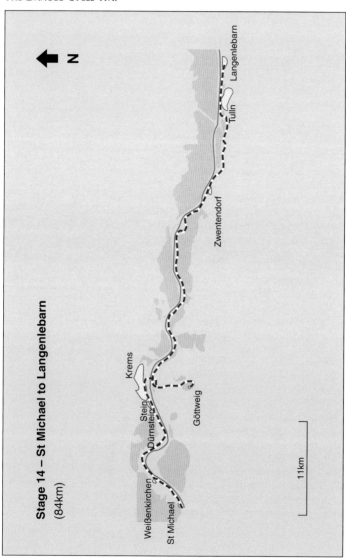

Stage 14 – St Michael to Langenlebarn
(84km)

Negotiate the cobbled main street busy with wandering tourists and leave the town through the arched gateway, crossing the main road immediately afterwards onto a country lane which continues to provide glorious views of terraced hillsides and fruit orchards.

Stein 205m (904/463)
Information, hotel, rooms
The thirteenth-century Minorite church, now used as the venue for exhibitions, has much to admire, as does that of St Nicholas and the old Frauenbergkirche which now serves as a war memorial. Although the town is something of a suburb of Krems there are some pleasant old houses tucked into narrow cobbled streets.

Krems 196m (908/459)
All facilities, campsite, cycle shop
Having entered via the imposing fifteenth-century Steiner Gate you will discover a very busy thousand-year-old university town with a wide main street lined with shops. Although not as immediately attractive as other towns you have recently visited on the route there are nevertheless a number of exceptional architectural delights.

The Baroque Church of St Viet is very imposing and the climb up the hill behind the town is rewarded with a visit to the fifteenth-century Piarist church with its decorated pillars. There are a couple of museums about local winemaking including the Municipal Wine Museum in the former Dominican church, which dates from the thirteenth century and was once a button factory and a theatre. The Gozzo Castle, more like a stately home, was also built in the thirteenth century and the town hall was constructed a century later.

To leave the town cycle to the Donau Bridge (well signed), turn right and cross it on the cycle lane. The cycleway swings hard right and although you are cycling in exactly the opposite direction from your destination, follow the signs as the trail dips away from the main road to a simple crossroads of tracks which contains clear signposting. Here turn left, away from the Donauweg, and set your sights on **Göttweig Abbey** sitting high up on a hilltop a few kilometres away.

Cycle into the village of **Palt** and then follow clear signs to the slightly larger village of **Furth**. Here the way is obvious as the abbey can be seen high above the road. The road begins to climb steeply, and where it bends to the left, take a right fork up through woods to the abbey. The climb is severe but not more than a couple of kilometres long. Emerge at the summit where the abbey provides interest and the restaurant sustenance.

Göttweig Abbey beyond Krems

Göttweig Abbey

'The Austrian Montecassino' as it is often called – was founded in the eleventh century as an Augustine monastery but by 1100 it had been handed over to the Benedictines. Places of special interest include the emperor's staircase, the princes' and emperors' rooms and the collegiate church. Whilst the abbey gives a fascinating insight into the affluent lifestyles of the monks, it is the view of the Donau flowing through the Wachau that always demands attention.

Having visited the monastery, zoom back down the hill and retrace the route as far as the crossroads of tracks encountered earlier but this time go straight ahead before the cycleway swings right and follows the right bank of the Donau again. For the next few hours the Donau is always at your side though the scenery is unspectacular and the cycleway bypasses towns rather than visits them. The result is a long but flat ride with few opportunities to rest. Keep an eye out for ropes stretched across the track – these are sometimes used to moor boats and are hazardous for the unwary cyclist!

Finally, as the Altenwörth power station comes into view, the route swings to the right away from the river and passes a *Radstation* with welcome food before crossing the River Traisen. Here swing left to regain the right bank of the Donau. Soon the surface of the trail becomes rougher for a while before crossing a footbridge and entering on tarmac the grounds of the unused Zwentendorf nuclear power station. The sight of lots of police is not sinister – part of the building is used as a police-training establishment!

In a short time the trail reaches the fringe of the town of

Zwentendorf 181m (951/416)
Information, guesthouse, rooms, campsite
A rough stretch of the cycleway leads along the bank of the Donau but where it is blocked and turns a right-angle to the right, the surface is paved and leads through the outskirts of the town to a chemical works. Cross the bridge and railway lines and head to the left into farmland away from the Donau. The trail is by no means straight here but is well signed through the hamlets of **Pischelsdorf** (campsite), **Langenschönbichl** and **Kronau** before arriving at the Große Tulln river. Cross this, and at a very unusual multiple junction avoiding the main road follow the signed trail heading for Tulln, taking care to keep off the huge bridge across the Donau. The trail follows the Große Tulln to its confluence with the Donau

where this very impressive bridge can be seen carrying the main road over the Donau.

Stay on the trail and shortly enter

Tulln 170m (966/401)
All facilities, campsite, cycle shop
This is a very ancient town reflected in its churches: St Stephen's (twelfth century) with a fine Romanesque West Portal, the Chapel of the Magi (thirteenth century), also with a fine portal, and the Minorite church (eighteenth century) which boasts a strangely decorated underground crypt.

There is an excellent Egon Schiele Museum in the old prison in which Schiele was once incarcerated, accused of producing pornography, and a Fire Brigade and Roman museum situated in the remains of the Minorite cloisters. The old market square is particularly attractive with buildings decorated in the Baroque style.

Shipbuilding used to be an important industry here. Unpowered barges were loaded and pushed out into the current where they floated downstream to their destination, then unloaded and broken up for firewood. This extravagant process ended when horse-drawn and then powered boats superseded them. Today the river here is still busy with commercial traffic and flotillas of hotel-boats which ply the river between Passau and Vienna.

Regain the cycle trail and cycle high up on the riverbank until you reach the town of

Langenlebarn 175m (971/396)
Information, rooms, shops, restaurant, guesthouses on road running parallel to right of cycleway

STAGE 15
Langenlebarn to Vienna (35km) – Total 1006km

This is a short half-day's ride. If you are planning to stay in Vienna give yourself plenty of time to find accommodation and explore the city.

Cycle back onto the riverbank and follow the well-marked cycleway along a dead-flat stretch of the Donau. A bar and children's play area near **Muckendorf** are the only things to disrupt this easy ride. The trail continues towards the dam and power station at Greifenstein. At the first opportunity take a well-signed right turn away from the river. This soon becomes an unsurfaced track that skirts an arm of the Donau leading directly into the riverside town of

Greifenstein 170m (981/386)
Information, hotel, rooms
There is a small twelfth-century castle which demands a steep climb to reach it but provides wonderful views along the Donau Valley and an inexpensive restaurant.

Regain the well-surfaced trail near the railway station, keeping the line on your right and the river on your left. It is common now to see houses lining the trail as you pass **Höflein**. You will also notice that the railway stations are becoming more frequent. At the exit from Höflein the trail leaves the river and heads inland, following the railway line along a tree-lined track. This continues into the very centre of

Klosterneuburg 168m (990/377)
All facilities, campsite
This very ancient town boasts two abbeys, the twelfth-century medieval one built on the site of a Roman fort and the Baroque abbey dating from 1730. There is also a twelfth-century abbey church which houses the Verdun Altar containing 51 panels of beautiful enamel work

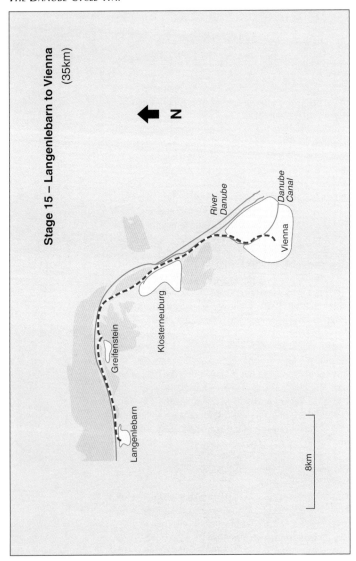

Stage 15 – Langenlebarn to Vienna (35km)

dated 1181. Added to this there is the twelfth-century Church of St Martin with its fantastic wooden statues.

There are a number of museums to be visited including one celebrating local history, the Abbey Museum and an archaeological museum. Away from the town centre are streets with tiny Weinstuben (wine bars) where a pleasant time can be spent sampling both the local wine and cuisine.

It is tempting to consider staying in Klosterneuburg and taking the frequent shuttle into Vienna to avoid the difficulties of finding accommodation in the Austrian capital. But be warned that this is an extremely busy and

Hundertwasser Tower and Danube Canal, Vienna

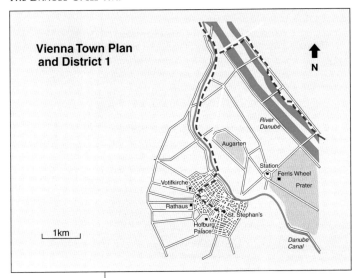

Vienna Town Plan and District 1

N

1km

River Danube

Augarten

Station

Ferris Wheel

Votifkirche

Prater

Rathaus

St. Stephan's

Hofburg Palace

Danube Canal

noisy town and quiet resting-places are at a premium. There is also little difference between the price of accommodation here and that of a similar standard in Vienna. (Note that the price of an overnight stay here is higher than if a stay of several days is booked.) The cycle ride into Vienna is pleasant and far more relaxing than negotiating the traffic in this hectic town centre.

As you arrive in Klosterneuburg pass left under the railway (take care at this extremely busy junction) and turn right in front of the campsite and tourist office on a well-signed minor road that quickly leads to the riverside cycleway. Soon this becomes lined with restaurants and bars where the Danube cruise ships tie up. Be sure to follow the signs carefully at the complex junction of roads and trails where the *Donauradweg* crosses the Donau Canal. Shortly after this DO NOT take the bridge to the left which crosses the Donau but cycle along the left bank of the Donau Canal through a pleasant waterside park past the magnificent incinerator chimney designed by Hundertwasser. This trail should be followed until the park finishes and the cycle track runs alongside the road.

Now cross the Donau Canal by the Augartem Bridge and immediately turn left to ride along the right bank of the canal. Any road to your right will now take you into the centre of

Vienna 165m (1006/361)
All facilities, youth hostels, campsites
It is worth spending several days here to absorb the splendour and character of this great city. It is a city on a grand scale so it takes time just to walk the length of some of the major streets. Cycle tracks are everywhere and the cycle is an excellent mode of transport in Vienna, especially for visiting some of the outlying sights.

District One – the Old Quarter – is in the very centre of the city with the Cathedral of St Stephen at its hub. Here can be found narrow cobbled streets and winding alleys cheek by jowl with the magnificence of Baroque architecture at its height. In District One you are as likely to be mown down by a horse and carriage as by a

The Anker clock, Vienna

Pulpit decoration in St Stephen's Cathedral, Vienna

Mercedes. One of the most fascinating little squares in the area is the Hoher Markt which houses the amazing Anker clock that springs to life at noon each day.

Around this district runs a double ring road which is well served with trams and cycle tracks. Beyond this is the residential and commercial area as well as the recreational zone of the city, known as the Prater, which contains the famous Ferris wheel. This huge area of land was bequeathed to the people of Vienna by the Emperor Joseph II and has been enjoyed by children and adults alike ever since. The area around the Ferris wheel is rather drab but the locals still patronise it in droves.

Vienna can be very expensive but it is well served by hostels and *Pensionen* that are no more expensive than those in the rest of Austria. Ask at the tourist information centres or at railway stations for lists of accommodation. A good map of Vienna is a must – these can be bought at most bookshops or information centres. Supermarkets can be found even in District One so meals do not have to be bought at expensive restaurants. It is worth spending some time in a Viennese coffee shop, however, where people come to read and

The Ferris wheel in the Prater, Vienna

think and meet like-minded folk – drinking the coffee is of secondary importance!

It is impossible to describe here all the places of interest in Vienna but the following are some of the high-lights. Do not miss the Cathedral of St Stephen or the Votifkirche. Their soaring architecture and their interiors are stunning. The carving of the figures on the pulpit of St Stephen's has to be seen to be believed! One of the most interesting views of the cathedral is its reflection in the ultramodern building opposite.

The Hofburg Palace and its attendant museums demand your time. Their proportions are massive and dwarf the viewer. The imperial treasury, known as the Schatzkammer, houses one of the most mind-blowing collections of medieval textiles and jewellery to be seen anywhere in the world.

The Spanish Riding School and the nearby stables in the Stallburg, Vienna's most famous Renaissance build-ing, plus the court apothecary which now houses the Lipizzaner Museum where the horses can be glimpsed through two portholes, are essential viewing.

The Belvedere which now houses an art gallery par-ticularly dedicated to the works of Gustav Klimt and Egon Schiele, and the seventeenth-century Schönbrunn Palace with its unique interior and formal Baroque gardens, should be seen if only to give perspective to the city. It is only here that a true skyline to the city can be appreciated.

The Prater district with its parks and huge Ferris wheel gives the Viennese the opportunity to unwind, and the Hundertwasser buildings, designed to brighten the lives of the poorer sections of Viennese society, are like nothing you have ever seen before. Enjoy a night's musical enter-tainment as well and you will have taken in enough of this fascinating city to make you want to return.

STAGE 16
Vienna to Bratislava (85km) – Total 1091km

There are many suggestions made by the local tourist offices as to which is the best way to leave Vienna for Budapest by cycle. Some of them are quick but others are extremely complicated, downright dangerous or illegal – 'Use the motorway, no-one will notice' was one piece of advice definitely not taken!

The simplest way is long and leisurely but none the worse for that. Return to the Donau Canal, cross to the far bank and retrace your entry journey as far as the motorway junction where a cycle trail is clearly signed *Donauweg* and turn right over the Donau itself on a wide dedicated cycle bridge. On reaching the far left bank drop down to the paved cycleway and cycle past a multitude of marinas, restaurants and bars with glimpses of Vienna beyond the island that stretches between the two banks. At this point it may startle you to know, in full flow, the Danube carries 14,000 cubic metres of water per second past this point!

Crossing the dedicated cycle bridge over the Danube, Vienna

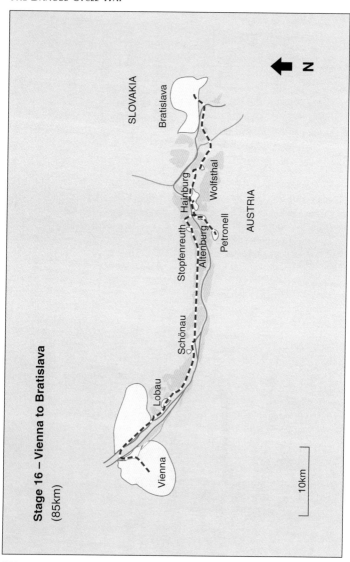

Stage 16 – Vienna to Bratislava
(85km)

At times there appear to be a number of cycleways all running parallel to each other and, to begin with, it does not matter which you take – the one nearest the water's edge is probably the best although it may be necessary occasionally to detour round restaurant tables or pedaloes pulled up out of the water! After passing beneath the motorway and railway bridges, however, taking the correct path becomes critical. Do not stay on the water's edge but climb to the top of the bank and take the track nearest the road to the left. When a huge chemical complex appears (Lobau) you must take a sharp left-hand turn and cycle through it, following the cycleway signs. This junction is very easy to miss and failure to find it will mean a long ride back to it, as there is no alternative route.

Once out of the chemical works the trail runs below the level of the levée but parallel to it, keeping it on the right-hand side. To the left side of the trail is fluvial forest. A long slow bend is now taken until a narrow bridge over a backwater leads to an embankment upon which the trail is clearly signed to 'Hainburg'. At this point you can see the village of

Schönau 153m (1031/336)
Guesthouse, snack bar

but is is not necessary to go through it. For another kilometre the trail swings past woodland to the right and then, with no warning, its nature changes completely. As far as the eye can see the trail is arrow straight on top of a high bank with woodland on either side. The key factor at this point is the wind, which can make this an exhilarating ride if it is in your favour but quite a grind if not as there are 12km of exposed cycling ahead!

Signs will be passed to **Orth** (*information, cycle shop, museums, castle, rooms*) and to **Eckartsau** (*information, Baroque castle, rooms*) but both can be ignored. Soon after the sign to Eckartsau the track surface deteriorates and begins to make a long sweep to the left.

Stopfenreuth 146m (1052/315)

Information, restaurant and bar, forestry centre
can provide sustenance if necessary before, after a kilometre, the trail passes beneath a high bridge that eventually crosses the Donau. Turn left off the trail here and climb up onto the bridge (take care as the cycleway is narrow and cross-winds are common) and cycle over the Donau into

Bad Deutsch-Altenburg 146m (1056/311)

Information, hotel, guesthouses, rooms, cycle shop
It is worth going to see the fourteenth-century church and the museum of Roman remains from nearby Carnuntum including a superb sculpture of Mithras killing a bull.

If you are interested in Roman remains take the road to the right to see some of the best preserved in the region 5km away at

Petronell-Carnuntum 180m (1061/306)

Information, hotel, guesthouse, cycle shop
This was a very large Roman camp housing upwards of 55,000 people. There are a number of sites to visit here including three amphitheatres, one of which could accommodate 8000 spectators, the remains of several buildings, some with mosaic floors and hypercausts, a triumphal arch, the Heidentor, and a rather down-at-heel castle as well as the Roman Museum which explains it all.

Having admired the Romans' handiwork return by the same road to Bad Deutsch-Altenburg, pass under the bridge that was crossed earlier and cycle on the right bank of the Donau until the cycleway arrives at the railway station at

Hainburg 145m (1068/299)

Information, hotel, guesthouses, rooms, campsite,
cycle shop
If possible enter the town by the great gateway, the Wienertor. The old town is ranged around the spacious

square. There is an interesting local history museum and a tobacco museum (you will pass the cigarette factory as you leave the town).

The exit from Hainburg is not clearly signed to Bratislava – sometimes called Pressburg. In fact the signs can be confusing or worse. Leave the bank of the Donau immediately after the station, turning right and keeping the railway line on your right. To begin with the route follows minor suburban roads lined with bungalows before swinging off left into farmland. At this point the high-rise apartments of Bratislava can be seen clearly away to the left. At the first T-junction, however, the cycleway turns sharp right to meet the railway line again and follows it on its left-hand side. In a couple of kilometres the same thing happens again but when the cycleway reaches the main road you have arrived in the hilly little village of

Wolfsthal 184m (1075/292)
Information, rooms
There is a ruined castle and a more modern (seventeenth-century) one, a pillory and a church worth visiting. This is the last village in Austria so make the most of it. Things are about to change!

Take the cycle track beside the main road until a formidable building straddles the road. This marks the border with Slovakia. Unsmiling armed border guards usher you through into a very different land beyond. What appears to be a cycle track runs along the left side of the main road.

Use it and then strike off the main road to the left as soon as possible onto a concrete cycleway through wasteland until the Donau (now called the Dunaj) is regained. Cycle on the right bank past semi-derelict amusement arcades, passing beneath two road bridges well adorned with graffiti and, at the next railway bridge, cross the river by means of a narrow cycleway alongside it (well used by both walkers and cyclists). You have now entered

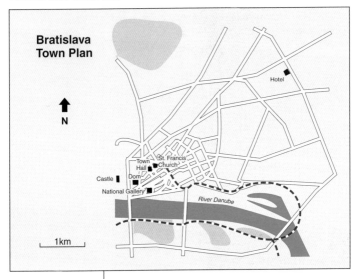

Bratislava Town Plan

↑ N

1km

Castle ▪
Town Hall ▪
Dom
St. Francis Church
National Gallery ▪
Hotel ▪

River Danube

Bratislava (Pressburg) 140m (1091/276)

All facilities, campsite

The less expensive hotels are to be found north of the Nivy district of the city. Unfortunately this entails cycling on busy, often dangerous and badly surfaced roads, negotiating tramlines, past densely packed, graffiti-covered towerblocks!

Street names are often written in Cyrillic script but this will not be found on street maps. Local people are not keen to talk or answer questions even in their own language. Do not expect them to speak English although hotel receptionists may speak a little.

Hotels are likely to ask you to surrender your passports during your stay. Currency may be a problem as Euros or dollars may only be accepted at a high rate of exchange and Slovakian krones are not easy to obtain out of the city centre.

The old quarter, though small, is very attractive with winding narrow cobblestoned streets and freshly painted Baroque buildings in bright colours. Artists and street

*Boy and bronze,
Bratislava*

performers are encouraged to work here and there are
some interesting and unusual sculptures.

There are a number of ancient churches and a clock
tower with a fine carillon. There are wine, clock and
pharmaceutical museums and the central square is lined
by buildings (some restored) with interesting architecture. The Primate's Palace with its impressive hall of mir-
rors should not be missed, nor should the Mirbach
Palace which houses an art gallery. Over the old quarter
broods the rebuilt ancient castle, the Hrad. This relatively
small tourist quarter is in very sharp contrast to the drab
city that surrounds it.

STAGE 17

Bratislava to Györladamér (76km) – Total 1167km

Return through the pot-holed streets of Bratislava to the River Dunaj and cross back to the right bank by the busy narrow bridge over which you entered (and which is still likely to be overcrowded). Drop down onto the cycleway and follow it as it swings to the left and climbs again, becoming very obvious on top of a high bank that affords extensive views of the Dunaj to your left, which now looks more like a series of huge lakes dotted with islands than a river. This is a popular recreation area for the people of Bratislava and the cycleway can be very busy in this area, particularly at weekends. The Dunaj continues to widen until the far bank can hardly be seen. Just beyond this point is an obvious crossroad of trails whose signs may cause some confusion.

Public transport in Bratislava

Ignore the signs (do NOT turn left along the obvious cycleway as is suggested) but turn right, dropping down

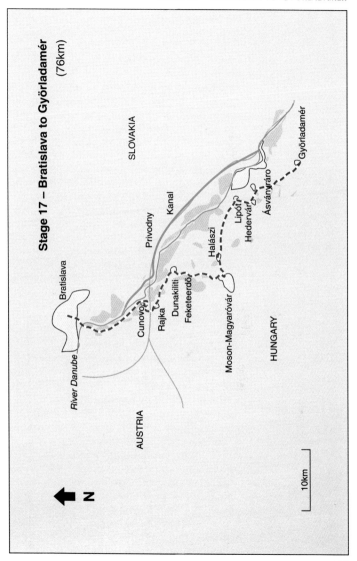

Stage 17 – Bratislava to Győrladamér
(76km)

N

to cross a small bridge over a stream, and cycle into the sleepy village of

Cunovo 133m (1109/258)
Guesthouse, rooms, bar

The village seems to be bereft of helpful signs but enquiries for *Ungarn* (Hungary) will elicit directions to the left through farmland. Soon a right-angle turn to the right needs to be made heading out to the main highway (Number 2). On reaching it turn left onto the highway and cycle alongside it as far as the brightly coloured border post between Slovakia and Hungary where you can change your currency into Hungarian forints. The rate may not be good but it may be the only opportunity to acquire forints during this stage of the route.

Once out of Slovakia the countryside takes on a more prosperous aspect with well-kept villages and brightly painted farms. The modes of transport, however, have now changed. The ubiquitous Mercedes, BMWs and Volkswagens of Germany and Austria have been superseded by noisy Skodas, Wurtburgs and Trabbants and these will soon be replaced in many places by horses and carts.

Cycle along the main road a short way beyond the border post and take the first road to the left (signed to Györ). It leads almost immediately into the sizeable village of

Rajka 129m (1114/253)
Hotel, rooms, bar (all with very low prices)

The cycleway is now along well-surfaced minor country lanes with little or no traffic – a dedicated cycleway is not necessary here. The countryside is either forested, with occasional roadside picnic places, or sown with maize. The water you may occasionally glimpse is a canalised section of the Dunaj known as the Mosoni Duna. It is not long before you reach the small country town of

Dunakiliti 125m (1122/245)
Rooms, campsite

Turn right in the centre in front of the church (still signed to 'Györ'). The cycleway is now well away from the river and will not return to its banks for the rest of this stage. In summer this region is given over to growing sunflowers, with fields of them stretching as far as the eye can see. Having passed through **Feketeerdö** the route now heads towards the large town of

Moson-Magyaróvár 127m (1133/234)

Information, hotels, guesthouse, rooms, campsite, cycle shop

This is the first sizable town on your route since leaving Bratislava and you may need to stock up with supplies or change money here. See the local Hanság Museum and Fireman's Museum as well as the charming old town and St László Church.

It is not necessary to cycle into the centre of town if you do not wish or need to. Having passed a modern church and graveyard on the right, take a well-signed road to the left towards **Halászi** which is reached after a pleasant flat ride of about 4km through level farmland.

Halászi 125m (1138/229)

Rooms, castle, railway museum

At the T-junction at the far side of town turn right onto the road to Ásványráro. Almost immediately follow a straight country trail to the left passing through the tiny picturesque villages of **Püski** after which the trail winds towards **Dunaremete** and

Lipót 117m (1149/218)

Guesthouses, rooms, campsite

There is a country leisure centre and lake which can be extremely busy with cars and pedestrians, especially at weekends.

Having passed the campsite take a sharp turn right and follow a country lane before picking up the main road again in

Hedervár 116m (1153/214)
No facilities
It is worth seeing the fine castle with Renaissance influences in its own grounds.

The road is now taken into the outskirts of the country town of

Ásványráro 116m (1156/211)
Rooms
See the church which is close to the road.

The way is now on a good dedicated cycle track alongside the road which gently undulates, leading through orchards and fields of maize and sunflowers with occasional farm hamlets. There is little traffic on the road that runs alongside the trail and, having passed through the small town of **Dunaszeg**, it is not long before the trail reaches

Györladamér 114m (1167/200)
Rooms, restaurant, bar

STAGE 18

Győrladamér to
Almásneszmély (88km) – Total 1255km

Although the route is approaching a large city it is not
unusual to find horse-drawn traffic on the road into
Győr. After passing through the villages of **Győrzámoly**
and **Győrújfalu** the road runs alongside a small stream
before passing a tiny supermarket (on the left) on the
approaches to

Győr 112m (1178/189)
All facilities, campsite, cycle shop
Sometimes known as the 'city of rivers' this fine Baroque
and neo-classical city manages to combine the old and
the new with great skill. There are several museums and
a spacious town square overlooked by the magnificent

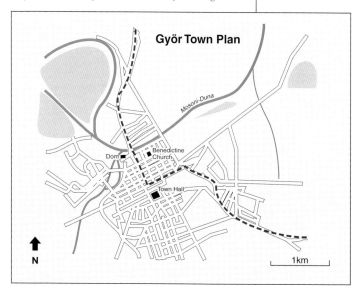

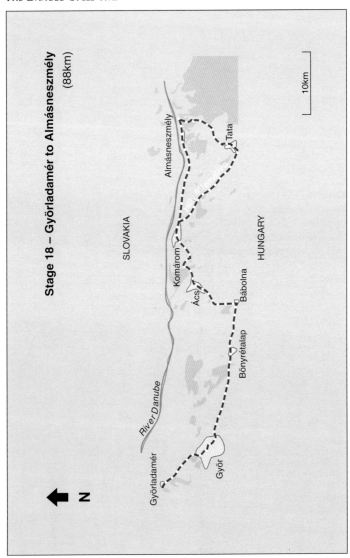

Stage 18 – Győrladamér to Almásneszmély
(88km)

10km

SLOVAKIA

HUNGARY

River Danube

Győrladamér

Győr

Bőnyrétalap

Bábolna

Ács

Komárom

Almásneszmély

Tata

N

town hall. One of the distinctive features of the city is the closed balconies at the corners of buildings. They are richly ornamented in a variety of forms.

Several of the churches are worth a visit, especially the Basilica where a beautifully sculptured reliquary of King Saint Ladislas can be admired. There is an interesting main shopping street and a tiny ancient quarter tucked away on the hillside.

Sculpture in Main Square, Györ

The exit from the town can be very tricky. It is advisable to ask for directions at the information bureau and to follow the route they suggest exactly – they will provide a map. Ask them to mark the way on it for you as you are unlikely to find any directional signs which will be of help here. The route leads through an estate of heavy industry, over busy road bridges with no cycle lanes and crosses the railway line amongst derelict buildings. Finally it emerges through light industry and swings to the left off the main road (signed) at a busy, dangerous junction soon after a second railway line has been crossed. Take great care throughout this section of the route as traffic is heavy and the road surfaces very poor.

After so much hectic cycling it is pleasant to pedal along empty roads again as the area known as the Szigetköz is approached. The cycleway climbs steeply at this point to cross a long flat hilltop, passing over the motorway before descending again through fields of maize and melons to

Bönyrétalap 131m (1199/168)
No facilities
The route is quite hilly now, passing through the village of **Bana** before it reaches the town of

Bábolna 140m (1206/161)
Information, rooms
This town, famous for its Arabian horses, has (as might be expected) a horse museum, and a stud farm founded in the eighteenth century which gives displays of horsemanship and husbandry and breeds the Arabian horses.

On leaving the town the road climbs steeply again before descending to cross the motorway for the second time. Soon afterwards it enters the peasant township of

Ács 116m (1216/151)
No facilities
Here there is still a distinct medieval atmosphere and

The hay harvest, Ács

you are more likely to be knocked off your cycle by a horse and cart than by a motor vehicle!

The town straggles along the road for some distance but where the houses finish the road surface turns to compacted soil (or mud depending on the weather) and sets off across farmland. For several kilometres now cycling is difficult, with deep ruts and overhanging branches to contend with, but do not be dismayed as, with no warning, the tarmac returns and the cycleway runs alongside a railway line. At the first junction after this turn right down a straight country lane and at the next T-junction take a 90-degree turn left and ride to the traffic lights in the centre of

Komárom 108m (1230/137)
Information, hotels, rooms, campsite
There is a Roman Catholic church, medicinal baths and the town hall to see. The main road is extremely busy and care must be taken here as there is no dedicated

cycle track. It is advisable to apply insect repellent here as the rest of this stage is renowned for its midges!

When the main road has been reached at the traffic lights in the town centre turn right onto it and cycle as far as **Szöny**, an industrial suburb of the town. The road remains very busy up to the point where the road to Tata turns off to the right. If you wish to go mountaineering take this road (it will join the recommended route again later) otherwise persevere along the road you are on until it crosses the railway line that has been running alongside the trail. At this point there is a cycleway of sorts provided though unfortunately it is made out of very uneven concrete blocks each only a couple of metres wide! This bumps its way along past derelict industrial buildings and chemical plants lining the banks of the Danube (now called the Duna in Hungary) which still cannot be seen at this point.

Immediately after **Almásfüzitö** turn left on a slightly more rural road (although still very busy) that runs parallel with the railway line, separating the cycleway from the Duna. Just beyond cycle into

Almásneszmély 110m (1255/112)
Bar, no facilities except at the high quality but expensive campsite which offers rooms, restaurant, bar, launderette, swimming pool (but no secure storage for cycles)
Just beyond the village ignore a road that climbs to the right advertising a hotel close by and cycle on to the large campsite mentioned above. Midges could be a problem here!

STAGE 19

*Almásneszmély to
Szentendre (86km) – Total 1341km*

Turn onto the riverside road, which is still busy, and cycle through the settlement of **Süttö** until the cycleway reaches the town of

Lábatlan 108m (1264/103)
No facilities
Again a choice presents itself here. A minor road can be taken to the right, which climbs steeply into the mountains, visiting Bajot and its nearby cloister, before returning to the main road which closely follows the river. Or ignore this diversion and stay by the river (no climbing necessary!) and the busy road soon leads into

Nyergesújfalu 106m (1269/98)
Shops but no cycleway or signs to it
Continue into the busy little town of

*Esztergom
from the basilica*

135

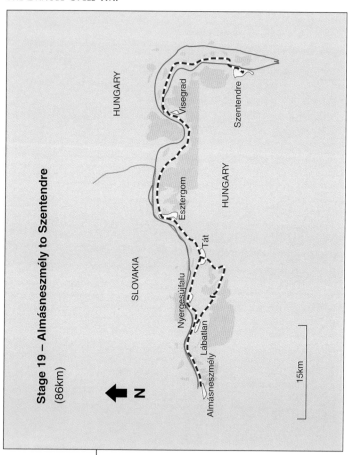

Stage 19 – Almásneszmély to Szentendre (86km)

Tát 102m (1277/90)
Bar, shops, plenty of horses and carts
Just after the road from Bajot rejoins from the right, take
a left fork on Road Number 11 clearly signed to

Esztergom 160m (1288/79)
Information, hotels, rooms, campsite, pool

Situated on the 'Golden Bend' of the Duna, this is one of the most famous towns along the river and therefore has its fair share of tourists.

It originated as a Roman town, was the birthplace and home of King Saint Stephen (he was crowned here in 1000) and was Hungary's capital for 250 years. The magnificent basilica towering above the town is the magnet for most visitors who want to see the Bakocz Chapel, the world-famous ecclesiastical collection in the treasury, the tomb of martyr Cardinal Mindszenty in the crypt and the Royal Palace.

There are a number of fascinating museums and palaces to see including the neo-Renaissance Primates' Palace housing the Christian Museum which contains paintings, sculptures, tapestries and goldsmiths' work from all over the world. For relaxation the cool waters of the thermal baths can be enjoyed.

There is a timeless atmosphere of faded glory about the town and the view of Slovakia, with its dull high-rise accommodation and industry on the northern bank of the river, serves to highlight this.

The official cycleway passes to the left of the basilica and hugs the riverbank. A much shorter and more pleasant route follows Road Number 11 (still relatively quiet here) which goes to the right of the basilica, climbing as it does so, before passing through pleasant market gardens and farms. The cycling is easy now with the road swinging away from the river to pass through **Pilismarót** (campsite) before regaining the riverbank at **Dömös** (campsite) whose Romanesque Provostal church boasts a fine crypt. To the right the view is dominated by a huge castle towering above the river and this is soon reached at the river and pleasant riverside town of

Visegrad (1313/54)
Information, hotel, guesthouse, rooms, campsite
The castle here was first built by the Romans, demolished by the Mongols and completed by Hungarian kings in the thirteenth century. It is far too high above the

road to contemplate a visit with laden cycles but at the edge of the town some of the remains run down to the lower castle beside the road. During the fourteenth century Visegrad became the seat of the Hungarian kings and remained so until the Turkish conquest. A Franciscan monastery was also built here. At that time most of the villagers were craftsmen at the royal court and lived outside its gates on the spot where the modern town now stands.

The town was resettled in the eighteenth century by South Germans who restored many of the houses. The town became prosperous as a port of call for shipping plying between Vienna and Budapest. Although the town has a rather 'down-at-heel' atmosphere there is still an attractive promenade and the famous thermal baths.

Soon after leaving the town look out for a small ferry to the left which plies its trade between the southern bank of the Duna and the island of Szentendrei Sziget. It runs infrequently and tends to moor on the island (wave and shout to the ferryman if necessary to catch his attention!), however a journey onto the island is very worthwhile as it is interesting and has a quiet, dreamy atmosphere.

On leaving the ferry turn sharp right along the only possible road. It passes through many stud farms and horse pastures. This is one of the main breeding and training areas for Hungary's famous horses and they will often be seen grazing the sparse grass that covers the island. Unfortunately where there are horses there are flies, so use your insect repellent!

Pass through the confusing centre of the little town of **Tahitótfalu** (ask for directions if necessary), not taking the ferry road but passing between numerous market gardens on a long straight road before turning sharp right as the outskirts of **Szigetmonostor** are reached to take the frequent car ferry back to the south bank of the Duna.

Once there turn left and follow the cycleway as it passes a large unprepossessing campsite before leading onto the raised promenade of the town of

Szentendre (1341/26)

Information, hotels, rooms, campsite, shops, restaurants, bars. If needed a list of places to stay can be found posted in the window of the tourist office at the far end of town although the office itself often seems to be closed. Hotels and guesthouses are to be found above the old town on the far side of the Road Number 11 bypass.

This town is famous for its Hungarian craft workshops. Coachloads of tourists from Budapest visit it every day to snap up 'bargains' and the old town has suffered as a result. However it is still an attractive place in the evenings and early mornings before the coaches arrive! The Serbian population who fled here from the Turks at the end of the seventeenth century have given the town a Mediterranean feel. There are a number of local museums and galleries though they are small scale (such as the Marzipan Museum). The Baroque Belgrade Cathedral and the Blagovestenska Church are worth visiting.

The Blue Craft Shop, Szentendre

STAGE 20

Szentendre to Budapest (26km) – Total 1367km

The exit from the town is not difficult to find but extremely tricky to negotiate! As soon as the town centre has been left behind you rejoin Road Number 11 which immediately becomes a fast and very busy highway. There are sporadic stretches of cycleway often changing from one side of the road to the other (take great care where this happens as many motorists in this area seem blind to cyclists and pedestrians). The surface of the cycleway can be uneven and uncomfortable to ride on but is infinitely preferable to jousting with the traffic on the main road hurtling towards the Hungarian capital!

The cycleway eventually drops below and away from the right-hand side of the road for a while and soon reaches the leisure complex at

Budakalasz (1347/20)
Snack bar, outdoor swimming pool
After passing the junction with the busy M2 road look out for a 90-degree turn to the left alongside a wide road leading past flats and small suburban shops. Take this turn, passing a large campsite where accommodation is available, to reach the river. Here turn right along a riverside track with a variable surface which runs past out-of-town hotels, bars and busy amusement arcades until just before a railway bridge. (The signage here is bad or nonexistent!)

Turn sharp right alongside a small tributary, cross it quickly, turn left again to regain the river, pass under the railway and turn sharp right again away from the river with the tributary and the railway on your right. If in doubt cycle at 90 degrees away from the river until you rejoin the Road Number 11 close to some Roman remains which include an aqueduct at Aquincum. This is part of a large and very interesting Roman Museum and is worth visiting at a later date if time allows.

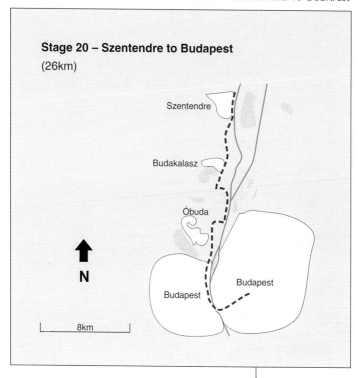

Road Number 11 can be extremely dangerous and it may be deemed safer to walk at this point. As soon as possible turn left off Road Number 11 to pass through the delightful suburbs of **Óbuda** with ancient stone houses and colourful squares filled with flowerbeds and statues of people sporting silver umbrellas.

Finally there is no alternative but to rejoin Road Number 11 yet again (turn left onto it). This is now a multi-laned highway with no provision for cyclists or pedestrians, and pushing a cycle seems more dangerous than riding it. The nightmare of cycling along this stretch of road (which includes negotiating a steep fly-over!) lasts for 2km before a new cycle lane appears alongside the tramlines, parallel to the River Duna. Follow this and admire the magnificent views of the Duna, its many bridges and the Parliament Buildings until the Elizabeth Bridge is reached.

Cross this bridge, which is the quietest of those spanning the Duna in Budapest, then cycle (or walk if the traffic is very heavy) along the road that stretches straight ahead until, in a kilometre, it arrives directly at the imposing International Keléti Railway Station. You are now in the very heart of

Budapest (1367/0)
All facilities, campsites
This cosmopolitan city where Eastern Europe meets Western is worth spending several days exploring. It has an air of faded grandeur with huge ornate buildings similar to those found in Vienna but whose facades are suffering from long-term neglect. Behind many of them are peaceful leafy courtyards now being converted into small shopping squares. They are a delight to enter, away from the noisy traffic-laden streets.

Statues with umbrellas, Obuda

Accommodation can be expensive in hotels near to the river or the main shopping centre but comfortable, clean *Pensionen* and hostels are available at low cost, particularly close to the international railway station (ask at the official tourist offices for details). It is worth shopping around before you decide where to stay. Ask to see the room and do not commit yourself unless you are satisfied that it has secure cycle storage, is what you want and what you are prepared to pay for.

Food and drink is cheap if purchased away from the main tourist centre. There are several supermarkets and inexpensive restaurants and bars close to the international railway station. Around Váci Utca prices are on a par with those found in other European capitals.

Unlike Vienna it is better to explore this city on foot rather than by cycle as the traffic is too heavy for comfort. There are no cycle lanes and few places safe enough to leave a cycle unattended. So leave your trusty steed hidden from view and securely padlocked to an immovable object at the place where you are

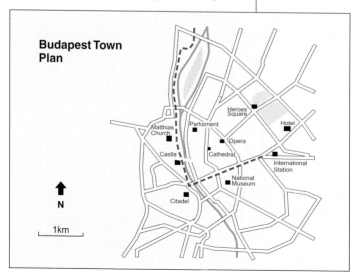

Budapest Town Plan

Heroes Square

Hotel

Matthias Church

Parliament

Opera

Castle

Cathedral

International Station

National Museum

N

Citadel

1km

*Courtyard off
Rákóczy, Budapest*

staying and take to the streets on foot, by tram or the underground.

Budapest is essentially a modern city founded when the towns of Óbuda, Buda and Pest were united in the late nineteenth century. The city burgeoned from that point, boasting the first underground railway in Europe as well as fine boulevards and grand international railway stations. The city continued to flourish until the Second World War when it was severely damaged. Since that time the ailing Communist regime was unable to restore it to its former glory and it is now struggling once more to climb the economic ladder to success.

The River Duna divides the city in two with Buda on the west side of the river and Pest on the east. The former is the historic quarter with elegant neo-classical buildings; the latter is the commercial and administrative centre. Both should be visited as they contain much of interest.

The hilly Buda boasts the Royal Castle begun in the fourteenth century by King Béla IV and extended during the Renaissance. It has been regularly damaged and then rebuilt until 1945 when it was burnt out. Today's rebuilding provides a cultural and historic tourist centre.

The Matthias Church in Holy Trinity Square is correctly known as The Church of Our Lady. The whole of

Fishermen's Bastion, Buda

Heroes' Square, Pest

the interior is covered in sumptuous paintings similar to those on the interior of Albi Cathedral in France and all is lit through beautiful stained glass.

There are incredible views of the whole of the city from the Fishermen's Bastion. This was probably part of Buda's original defence works. This whole area is a maze of medieval streets and alleyways in which it is a pleasure to become lost. Any downhill road will lead eventually to the river. Here there are plenty of benches from which to admire the Parliament Buildings and watch the river traffic passing by.

The flatter Pest is quite different in both looks and architecture. It has Heroes' Square close to the rather bedraggled City Park, the enormous neo-classical Parliament Buildings built at approximately the same time – the turn of the twentieth century – and the fashionable and very expensive Váci Utca shopping area. The latter helps to provide the Hungarian capital with the rather extravagant title of 'the Paris of Eastern Europe'. The State Opera House can genuinely stand comparison with any similar building in Europe. Its golden stone façade is very beautiful and its interior is sumptuous. A visit to the opera here is a truly memorable occasion. The National Gallery and the Hungarian National Museum contain works of exquisite beauty and the Cathedral of King Saint Stephen containing the enormous marble statue of its patron saint is one of the main centres of the Catholic Church in Hungary.

When you have exhausted all of these there are 223 museums in the Hungarian capital, 40 theatres, seven concert halls, two opera houses and hundreds of cultural events! You will simply be spoiled for choice.

The most fascinating place, however, is none of these but the Grand Market where every conceivable thing Hungarian is sold on its two colossal floors. A vast array of market stalls in serried ranks serve huge crowds of locals and a few tourists with everything they could possibly imagine. The sights, sounds and smells here will linger long after the main tourist sights have faded.

Be aware that Budapest suffers from a great deal of petty crime. Pickpockets abound in the busy tourist areas including the bustling Grand Market and beggars operate throughout the city. The latter can be very persistent and children have a habit of attaching themselves to your

Grand Market, Pest

Statue of King Saint Stephan, Buda

clothing and refusing to let go until their demands have been met. All this of course takes place under the watchful eye of their parents!

If at the end of the day you want to relax and take the strain out of those tired muscles, a visit to the Gellért, Rudas or Széchenyi Medicinal Baths will soak away your aches and pains. You can even stand in the water and play chess, as many Hungarians do, on floating chessboards.

For a little peace after all the noise and bustle that is everywhere in this busy metropolitan city, Margaret Island is a haven. Standing in the middle of the Duna and served by two sets of bridges it is a nature park and recreation area with very little traffic. On this shady island you can amble or laze under the shade of leafy trees with the cooling breezes off the Duna to fan you to sleep. You deserve your rest!

BIBLIOGRAPHY

Andrea Achulte-Peevers, Jeremy Gray & Anthony Haywood, *Germany*. Australia: Lonely Planet, 2000
A general overview of the country with excellent descriptions of some of the main cities to be visited and a short piece on the Danube Cycle Way.

Langdon Faust, *Austria, The Complete Guide*. United States: Fodor, 1998
Similar in layout to the above with a long comprehensive section on the Danube Valley including all the main city guides and town plans. (This and the above are too heavy to take on the journey.)

Bob Ordish, *German for Travellers*. Bielefeld: Peter Rump, 1988
An excellent easy-to-carry pocketbook which contains all the essential phrases a cyclist might need along the way and a great deal more.

Art Guide No. 41, *Cathedral of Regensburg*. Regensburg: Schnell & Steiner, 1999
A well-illustrated and inexpensive pocketbook detailing the history and architecture of one of Germany's most beautiful cathedrals.

Wolfgang Kootz, *Passau – The Three Rivers City*. Ubstadt-Weiher: Kraichgau, 2000
A detailed guide to the city. It includes a number of suggested walks, taking in the most important sites (and sights) in and around Passau.

Brigitte Teutsch, *Vienna City Guide*. Innsbruck: Kompass, 1999
An excellent, if rather heavy, little guide containing maps, illustrations, suggested sightseeing routes and a geographical and historical background to Austria's capital.

Rózsa Szalontay, *Budapest*. Budapest: Szalontai Publishing House, 2000
A pleasantly illustrated guide to the city, which is too big to fit in a pocket. Good pocket guides are difficult to find but this is perfectly adequate if you are on foot.

Reinhard Steiner, *Schiele*. Köln: Taschen, 2000
A beautifully and comprehensively illustrated book on the life and works of the celebrated Austrian artist who lived and worked in Tulln, where there is a small museum of his life.

THE DANUBE CYCLE WAY

Philip Mattson, *Hundertwasser KunstHausWien*. Köln: Taschen, 1999
A remarkable insight into the theories behind the architecture of this outstanding Viennese artist. It is beautifully illustrated and contains a large number of quotes from Hundertwasser himself. This is worth reading before visiting any of Hundertwasser's buildings.

József Vadas, *Hungarian Art, a Brief History*. Budapest: Corvina, 1998
This lavishly illustrated book points out the location of many of Hungary's most important artworks, many of which are to be found in Budapest or along the Danube Valley.

MAPS

J. Crasemann, *The Danube from Donaueschingen to the Black Sea*. Lübeck: Schöning & Co, 2000
This is a diagrammatic map of the Danube Valley with a number of illustrations and paragraphs about the main features of the river. (It should not be used for navigation purposes.)

Germany No. 984 (1:400,000). Watford, UK: Michelin, 2000
Hungary No. 925 (1:400,000). Watford, UK: Michelin, 2000
These two maps are good for route planning but do not carry enough detailed information to be of much use on the Danube Cycle Way.

Radwandern von Donaueschingen bis Passau. Austria: Bikeline, 1998
Danube Bike Trail – Passau to Vienna. Austria: Bikeline, 1998
Donau-Radweg – Von Wien nach Budapest. Austria: Bikeline, 1999
These three guides provide excellent large-scale maps of the Danube Cycle Way with the route clearly shown. However the text in the first and third volumes is in German and that in the second volume is a direct translation from the German language into English and is not easy to follow.

APPENDIX A

Suggested Accommodation

Donaueschingen
Naturfreundehaus
Alte Wolterdinger Straße 72
78166 Donaueschingen
Tel. 0771 2985

Stetten
Walter & Irmgard Löffler
Blumenstraße 12
D 78570 Mülheim Stetten
Tel. 07463 7680
Ennetach

Otto Kirchbauer
Keltenweg 2, Ennetach
88512 Mengen
Tel. 07572 5288
Dettingen

Donaustuben
Höllweg 5
Dettingen
Tel. 07391 8916

Günzburg
Naturfreundehaus
Schmiedlweg 2
89312 Günzburg
Tel. 08221 6103/34944
Altisheim

Landgasthof Grünenwald
Hopfenweg 4
86687 Altisheim
Tel. 09097 266

Landershofen
Ilse Halbig
Am Haselberg 15
85072 Eichstätt-Landershofen
Tel. 08421 7793

Dietfurt
Gasthof zur Post
Hauptstraße 25
92345 Dietfurt
Tel. 08464 321

Weltenburg
Anna Schabmüller
Zieglerweg 6
Weltenburg
Tel. 09441 5301

Rosa Brunner
Pater Josefstraße 5
93309 Kelheim-Weltenburg
Tel. 09441 10242
Kirchroth

Gasthaus Lacke
Kirchroth b. Straubing
Tel. 0 94 28/3 24

Passau
Rotel Inn Der Ruhende Mensch
Hbf./Donauufer
94012 Passau
Tel. 0851 95160

Hinding
Familie Bachl
Hinding 43
4785 Haibach
Tel. 07713 8202

Puchenau
O & E Kepplinger
Großambergstraße 17
A-4048 Puchenau
Tel. 0732 221759

Linz
Goldenes Dachl
Hafnerstraße 27
Linz
Tel. 775897

Grein
Pauckner
Groißgraben 1
A-4360 Grein an der Donau
Tel. 07268 7550

C. Schlossgangl
Groißgraben 3
A-4360 Grein an der Donau
Tel. 07268 7308

St Michael
Maria-Theresia & Erich Wangler
A-3610 Weißenkirchen/Wachau
Wösendorf 65
Tel. 02715 2337

Weißenkirchen
Alida Rammel-Graf
Kremser Straße 218
3610 Weißenkirchen
Tel. 02715 2340

Langenlebarn
Gerlinde Weidlinger
Tullnerstraße 48
3425 Langenlebarn
Tel. 02272 62568

Vienna
Pension Samwald
Hörlgasse 4 , 1090 Vienna
Tel. 317 74 07

Bratislava
Hotel Turist
Ondavská ut. 5
PO Box 128
820 05 Bratislava
Tel. 00421 7/5557 2789

Györladamér
Fortuna Gasthaus
Ungarn Györladamér
Arany ut. 2
Tel. 0036 96352225

Neszmély
Camping Eden
an der Hauptstraße Nr 10
2544 Neszmély Pf. 7
Tel. 0633 474183

Szentendre
St Andrea Fogadó
2000 Szentendre
Egressy ut. 22
Tel. 26 311 989

Budapest
Dominik Panzio
Cházár András ut. 3
Tel. (36-1) 343 7655

APPENDIX B
Full Kit List

Cycle lights

Folding spare tyre, puncture repair outfit, spare inner tubes

Water bottles, steel thermos that fits into bottle cage

Cycle computer

Cycle locks

Cycling gloves

Cycling glasses (tight fitting)

Helmets

Tools including Allen keys and plastic tape

Spare spokes, Swarfega, thin disposable plastic gloves

Pump

Velcro straps

Dog-dazer

Mini electric kettle

Mending kit

First aid kit

Insect repellent

Army knife

Scissors

Lighter

Tissues

Polythene bags

Cutlery

Plates

Cups

Dishcloth

Scourer

Universal plug

Stretch line

Washing-up liquid

Clothes washing liquid

Mini cool bag

Maps

Guides

Dictionaries

Camera

Films

Mini binoculars

Dictaphone

Passport

E111

Currency

Credit cards

Debit cards

Spectacles

Sun glasses

Pen & pencil

Notebook

Toothbrush

Tooth gel

Shower gel

Fibre towels

Toilet roll

Sun cream

Lip salve

Clothes

Thermals

Pertex jackets

Waterproof clothing

Spare shoes

Sleeping bags

Pocket pillows

Glucose tablets

Isostar sachets

Coffee, tea bags etc.

Dried milk

Sugar cubes

Emergency dried meal

APPENDIX C
Useful Addresses

Cyclists Touring Club
Cotterell House
69 Meadrow
Godalming
Surrey GU7 3HS
Tel. 01483 417217
website www.ctc.org.uk

Cotswold Outdoor Equipment
Unit 5, Corinium Centre
Love Lane
Cirencester GL7 1YJ
Tel. 01285 643434

Dog-Dazer
204 Broadway
Peterborough PE1 4DT
Tel. 0171 228 2360

European Bike Express
31 Baker Street
Middlesbrough
Cleveland TS1 2LF
Tel. 01642 251440
email: bolero@bolero.demon.co.uk

Stanford's Map Shop
12 Long Acre
Covent Garden
London WC2
Tel. 0207 836 1321

Trek Bicycle Corporation Ltd
Maidstone Road
Kingston,
Milton Keynes MK10 0BE
Tel. 01908 282 626

Ortlieb Bags
Lyon Equipment
Rise Hill Mill
Dent, Sedbergh
Cumbria LA10 5QL
Tel. 015396 25493

Coolmax Socks
Ridgeview Inc
PO Box 8
NC 28658
USA
Tel. 001 704 464 2972

TOURIST OFFICES
Austrian National Tourist Office
30 St George St
London W1R 0AL
Tel. 0171 629 0461
email Oewlon@easynet.co.uk

Hungarian Tourist Office
46 Eaton Place
London SW1X 8AL
Tel. 0171 823 1032
email htlondon@hungarytourism.hu

German National Tourist Office
Brochure Ordering Service
London W1
Tel. 0900 1600 100

Basle Tourist Office
Schifflände 5, Basel
Tel. 0041 61 268 68 68
email info@baseltourismus.ch

Budapest Tourist Office
PO Box 215
1364 Budapest
website www.budapestinfo.hu

Donaueschingen Tourist Office
Karlstraße 58
D-78166 Donaueschingen
Tel. 0049 771/857 221
email stadt@donaueschingen.de
website www.donaueschingen.de

Eichstätt Tourist Office
Kardinal Preysing Platz 14
85072 Eichstätt
Tel. 08421 98 80 0
website www.eichstaett.de

Grein Tourist Office
Stadtplatz 7
A-4360 Grein
Tel. 07268 7055
website www.tiscover.com/grein

Györ Tourist Office
Aradi vértanuk ut. 22
H-9021 Györ
Tel. 0036 96 11 557; 0036 96 17 601

Klosterneuburg Tourist Office
PO Box 37
Klosterneuburg
Tel. 02243 343 96
email tourismus@klosterneuburg.com

Linz Tourist Office
Urfahrmarkt 1
PO Box 117, A-4040 Linz
Tel. 732 70 70 1777
website www.tiscover.com/linz

Passau Tourist Office
Neues Rathaus
Rathausplatz 3
94032 Passau
Tel. 0851 95598 0

Melk Tourist Office
Babenberger Straße 1
A-3390 Melk
Tel. 43 2752 52307 32
website www.melk.gv.at

Szentendre Tourist Office
Dumtsa Jeno ut. 22
Szentendre 2000
Tel. 36 26 317 965

Vienna Tourist Office
Obere Augartenstraße 40
A-1025 Wien
Tel. 21114 0

APPENDIX D
Glossary of Terms (English–German)

CYCLING

bottle	*Flasche*
brake	*Bremse*
cable	*Drahtseil*
chain	*Kette*
cycle	*Fahrrad, Rad*
cycleway	*Radweg*
gear	*Getrieb*
grease	*Schmiere*
handlebars	*Lenkstange*
helmet	*Helm*
nut	*Schraubenmutter*
oil	*Öl*
pump	*Pumpe*
puncture	*Loch*
pedal	*Fahren*
saddle	*Sattel*
spanner	*Schraubenschlüssel*
speed	*Gang*
spoke	*Speiche*
tyre	*Reifen*
wheel	*Rad*

OTHER

accident	*Unfall*
bakery	*Bäckerei*
break	*Brechen*
bridge	*Brücke*
castle	*Burg/Schloss*
church	*Kirche*
city	*Großstadt*
direction	*Führung*
door	*Tür*
field	*Feld*
garage	*Garage*
guesthouse	*Gasthof, Pension*
house	*Haus*
inn	*Gasthaus*
main road	*Hauptstraße*
map	*Karte*
motorway	*Autobahn*
railway	*Eisenbahn*
river	*Fluß*
rooms	*Zimmer*
square	*Platz*
street	*Straße*
supermarket	*Supermarkt*
tourist information office	*Fremdenverkehrsbüro*
town hall	*Rathaus*
wine bar	*Weinstube*
youth hostel	*Jugendherberge*

LISTING OF CICERONE GUIDES